EVERY CHILD'S
BOOK OF
RIDING

Edited by

JENNIFER AND DORIAN WILLIAMS

BURKE ★ LONDON

ACKNOWLEDGEMENTS

The Publishers and the Editor wish to thank the following for permission to reproduce photographs:

Bucks Herald, Rex Coleman, Fox Photos, Graphic Photos, Peter Harding, Jamie Hodgson, International News, Keystone Press Agency, L. G. Lane, J. E. L. Mayes, Mirrorpic, Monty, National Coal Board, Photonews, Planet News, Reed Photography, Sport & General, John Watkins, Charles White

222 69016 X

Burke Publishing Co. Ltd.
14 John Street, London, W.C.1
Printed in Great Britain by
Fleming and Humphreys (Baylis) Ltd., Leicester

EVERY CHILD'S
BOOK OF
RIDING

EVERY CHILD'S AMBITION   *To be presented by the Duke of Edinburgh with the rosette as winner of the Pony Club Mounted Championship—Horse of the Year Show*

Contents

PAGE

Introduction 9

CHAPTER

1 BUYING A PONY Jimmy Younghusband 11
Type · Cost · How to find one · Ponies on trial · Testing a pony · Vetting · The best age · Native breeds.

2 LOOKING AFTER A PONY Jennifer and Dorian Williams . . 17
The field · Fencing · Shelter · Feeding · Watering · The pony at work · The pony living in · Out at grass · Regular supervision.

3 SIMPLE STABLE MANAGEMENT Jennifer Williams . . . 22
The stable · Door, Window, Drains, Floor · Looking after the stable · Bedding · Forage · Grooming · Tack · Clothing.

4 SIMPLE SCHOOLING Jennifer and Dorian Williams . . . 33
Patience · Titbits · Tying up · The mouth · Obedience · Seat · Legs · Hands · Aids · The Voice · Walk · Trot · Canter · Halt · Rein back · Temperament · *Cavaletti* · Simple jumping · A lane · Parallel poles · Doubles and trebles · Impulsion · Competitions · Seat and hands for jumping · Balance.

5 MINOR AILMENTS Jennifer Williams 49
The medicine cupboard · Fomentations · Tubbing · Hosing · Wounds and cuts · Anti-tetanus · Saddle sores and girth galls · Cracked heels · Windgalls · Capped hocks and elbows · Sidebones and ringbones · Sprains · Colic · A pony in good condition.

6 NATIVE PONY BREEDS Mrs I. M. Yeomans 56
Connemaras · Dartmoors · Dales · Exmoors · Fells · Highlands · New Forest · Shetlands · Welsh.

7 PIT PONIES Bill Ackroyd 66
Facts and figures · Types of ponies · Stabling · Fun and games · Illness · Miners' affection for their ponies · Age and retirement · Working hours · Legal safeguards.

8 THE RIDING SCHOOL Douglas Mould 74
Locality · Type of pony · Feeding · Breaking · Voice · Pupils · Routine.

9　THE GYMKHANA PONY　Colonel Jack Bullen　.　.　.　.　81
Origin · Prince Philip Cup · Good all-round pony · Training · Rewards · Hints for riders · Good condition · Suitable events.

10　THE PONY CLUB　Christine Black　.　.　.　.　.　88
Origin · Membership · Local branches · Rallies · Camps · British Horse Society; its objects.

11　GREAT EQUESTRIAN EVENTS　B. L. Kearley　.　.　.　.　98
The Olympic Games · Badminton · Burghley · Pony Club Championships · The White City · The Horse of the Year Show · The Classic races · The Grand National · The Westchester Cup.

12　SHOW JUMPING ON TELEVISION　Dorian Williams　.　.　.　112
What to look for · Different styles · The experts · Behind the scenes · The producer · The cameras · The commentator.

Conclusion　.　.　.　.　.　.　.　.　.　.　128

Introduction

Nowadays, more and more children want to have a pony of their own. Many more just want to ride, hoping that they may sometimes be able to borrow a pony. Most of them are not able to get good instruction and those who take lessons can usually only ride once or twice each week—and that does not even apply to all seasons of the year. So even those lucky ones who have a pony and can get good instruction sometimes find it very difficult to remember everything they are taught, whether it is about riding, grooming or feeding a pony, or any of the many other things which you have to know if you are going to deal with ponies.

Every Child's Book of Riding is designed to help fill in the gaps. It is a book to have by you, a book to turn to when you find you have forgotten some little point which you ought to know about how to handle your pony. The book is divided into sections with pictures and diagrams so that you will quickly and easily be able to look up whatever subject it is you particularly want to know about.

You may not want to read the book straight through from cover to cover as if it were a story book, but if you do you will find that by the time you reach the end of the last chapter you may well have forgotten some of the advice and information which was in the first chapter. This is, of course, only natural as the book contains a vast amount of detail on all aspects of riding and will serve as a handbook over a long period of time, rather than a book which only holds your interest for a few days and to which you never return.

Perhaps you have never had any instruction at all from an expert teacher; it may be that a friend has suddenly said that you may ride his or her pony or that you have been given a pony as a gift. If you follow the different chapters of this book carefully you will not go far wrong, because they include all the *basic essentials* on riding and horse-mastership.

There are books, much larger than this, written on the many finer aspects of horsemanship; perhaps you will soon be needing them, but in the meantime this book deals with the simple and elementary rules and facts, and that is all it is intended to do.

Every Child's Book of Riding really falls into two parts: the chapters on instruction and the chapters of more general interest, such as the one on pit ponies, or the great equestrian events. We have included these in our book because we feel that the true horse-lover should have some knowledge beyond his or her own pony. Did you know, for instance, that there are still 10,000 ponies working in the mines in Britain; that there are over 40,000 members of the Pony Club; that Welsh *Mountain* Ponies must not be more than 12 hands, but that *Welsh* Ponies can be up to 13 hands 2 inches; that the *classic* races, of which the Derby is the most important, are for three-year-olds?

Incidentally, I wonder if you know the difference between a horse and pony? It is often difficult to tell because sometimes a horse has pony blood in it, like Sheila Wilcox's *High and Mighty*, whose eel stripe down his back (that black line from mane to tail that you sometimes see on bay or dun ponies and horses) shows he has Connemara blood in his veins; and, of course, good pony mares are often mated with real horse stallions. But, as a general rule, if a pony is over 14 hands 2 inches (there are 4 inches in a hand: roughly the breadth of a man's hand) then he is said to be a horse.

A real horse- or pony-lover ought to know such things; and you will find them all in the chapters of this book.

One thing you will not find, because it does not really fit into any particular chapter, is advice about clothes for riding. I am sure it is wrong to think that you can only ride if you have expensive clothes. For riding at home, jeans are quite good enough. For a riding school or a gymkhana, jodphurs can often be acquired second hand from someone who has grown out of them as quickly as you will. Riding in soft shoes is always uncomfortable, but there is no need to buy special shoes for riding, an ordinary pair of walking shoes is ideal. The one absolute essential is a hard cap. Hundreds of bad accidents are avoided every year by the use of a hard cap.

My wife and I have been with horses and ponies all our lives—I think I first rode before I was three!— and fell off! We have also been lucky enough to know many of the outstanding people in the different branches of the horse world. We have tried to compress into this book all those facts, experiences and opinions which we believe will be of most help to you.

We very much hope that you will enjoy it.

Jennifer + Dorian Williams

CHAPTER ONE

Buying a Pony

JIMMY YOUNGHUSBAND

TYPE · COST · HOW TO FIND ONE · PONIES ON TRIAL ·
TESTING A PONY · VETTING · THE BEST AGE · NATIVE
BREEDS

Since children have become so interested in horses and ponies again far more people want to buy ponies than ever before. Having watched Pat Smythe on television, or perhaps a series such as we recently did on "Studio E", literally hundreds of children write to us asking: "How can I buy a pony?" This is a very difficult question to answer, because so much depends on different circumstances. Obviously children living in a town have very different needs from those living in the country. An experienced rider will need something quite different from a beginner.

Jimmy Younghusband has been buying horses and ponies all his lifetime: not only for his school at Stanmore and for private customers, but also for films, for which he provides hundreds of horses each year. We have asked him to give us a few useful hints on how to buy a pony. Editors

A YOUNG child who is keen on riding longs to possess a pony. One of the present day problems is how to set about it.

I want to advise both parents and young people that buying a pony is not a thing to be treated lightly. After many years' experience in this matter, and having been "had" on more than one occasion in days gone by, I would first ask:

1. What type of pony are you looking for?

2. How much can you afford to pay for it?

3. How do you go about looking for it?

Let us begin with the first problem. Ponies can be roughly divided into three classes, show ponies, hunting ponies, and gymkhana ponies. It is no use buying a show pony unless you are a pretty competent rider, and have the opportunity to attend shows regularly; also they are expensive. A winner at one of the very big shows would cost several hundred pounds; a winner at local shows, any price up to two hundred pounds. So, unless you are a very fortunate young person this type of pony is out of the question.

Ponies used for hunting are in a class on their own. Lots of ponies are perfect hacks, but too keen when out hunting; so remember, before buying this type insist on having a day's hunting on him, to see if he can jump, and that you can "hold" him.

Gymkhana ponies need only be handy, with good mouths and an ability to jump a little.

The next important question is how much should you pay. It is nearly impossible to state a fixed price, so much depends on the pony's manners, ability and looks. Prices today are not cheap, and one must be prepared to pay anything from sixty to one hundred pounds for an ordinary pony. The price is governed by the pony's age and soundness, and other points I have already mentioned.

Now the last and most important question, where to buy the perfect pony. There are very few about, but my advice to you is, make inquiries amongst your friends, and find out if they know of anyone who, for a genuine reason, has a pony to sell; the type of pony you want to buy. This does not often happen, so you must often go to someone who deals in ponies, and can offer you a choice of several.

If you are a teenager, thirteen or thereabouts, remember you can grow several inches in a year or two, so you want a pony 13 hands to 14 hands 2 inches. If you buy a smaller one you may have the sorrow of having to sell the pony in a year or two, unless you have brothers and sisters younger than yourself, who will then be the right size to ride him.

There are many people who deal in ponies and are quite honest; but all trades have a few rogues, so take precautions before you set out to buy. If you contact organizations like the British Horse Society, the Association of British Riding Schools, or (if you live in the South of England) the Horse Lovers' Agency at Standlake in Oxfordshire, they will all be quite willing to help you.

Sometimes one is asked: "Can I have the pony on a week's trial?" the answer generally is "No", and the dealer is quite right, especially if he does not know you. If you are a bad horseman you can knock pounds off the value of the pony in a week's riding. Most dealers will let you come to their place of business and, for a small fee, ride the pony every day for a short period.

Here are some important things to remember when buying a pony:

Make sure the pony is not "nappy"; take him out of his yard, trot him down the road, then turn and trot him back past his own

NEW FOREST PONY SALE *You will need a good eye for a pony to select the best one from a bunch like this*

yard entrance several times; if he does not play up you can be fairly sure he is not nappy.

Test him for a "kicker" by riding him close to several other ponies for a few minutes, and see if he shows resentment, then make him leave the crowd and go off by himself; if he does this willingly it is a good test for manners.

Take the pony out in the open country with others, canter him down hill, and see if you can hold him.

Pick up all four feet and tap the shoes with a hammer; some horses refuse to be shod without fighting and have to be "twitched" which is a bad thing.

One very important point; if the pony is to live out of doors, turn him out in a field with other ponies, and then go out with a halter and a tin of oats, catch and bring him in. If he refuses to be caught you may have trouble in store.

If he lives in the country, ride him along a road where there is lots of

BAMPTON FAIR, DEVON *A young pony with a will of his own: but remember that although he looks strong, if you buy a colt like this, only a few months old, you must be very patient and not attempt to ride him for at least two years*

heavy traffic, you will soon find out if he is traffic shy.

Finally, before you buy the pony get him checked by a qualified veterinary surgeon who understands horses and who will tell you the age of the pony (you would be well advised not to buy a pony under three or four years of age) and whether he is sound and likely to remain so with fair treatment.

Lots of people seem to think that you must buy a young pony, and that a pony nine or ten years old is worn out and finished. This is not so; with reasonable care, a pony or small cob will do his job until he is nearly twenty. If one has eight or ten years' faithful service out of a pony, what is there to complain about? Also remember that a young pony of four years old is not fully developed. All his bones and muscles are not yet near the hard stage, so unless you ride him very lightly for a year or two, he will develop splints (which cause lameness) and other strains.

Young people, especially teenagers, often buy a nearly clean-bred pony, whose sire is a thoroughbred, and his

14

BARNET FAIR: *one of the oldest in the country*

dam nearly so, because they look pretty and full of life. This is all right if you are a fairly experienced horseman, can afford to keep your pony in the stable, feed him properly all the time and *give him plenty of regular exercise*. If you are a youngster who goes to school and can only ride your pony at week-ends, and sometimes not even then, buy a good native pony, whether he is Welsh, Dartmoor, Exmoor or any other native breed; you will not go far wrong if you buy the very best type of one of these breeds. They are not cheap today, but they are worth buying.

This type of pony is used to living out (thereby exercising himself) and, if you are riding every day, a little corn feed twice a day would be necessary.

Native breeds as a rule are reasonably placid and do not hot up. They carry good condition under all circumstances, and do not quickly lose weight like blood ponies.

I know there are exceptions to every rule, but this is the case with the average pony.

Next problem: what do you look

15

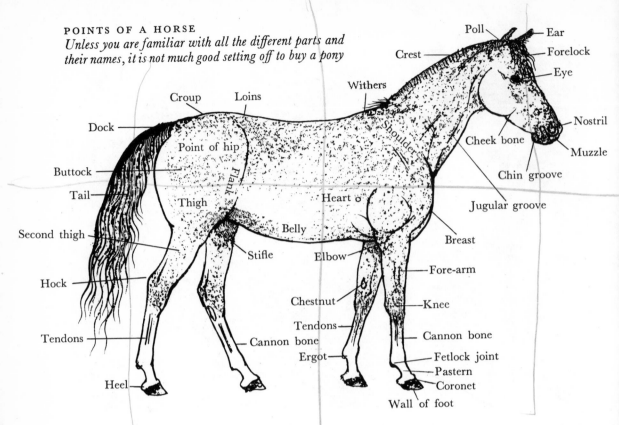

for in a pony that you are going to ride fairly hard (in the holidays anyway)? First of all he must have well-shaped feet, not too flat, not too round like a donkey's and strong enough to carry him. He must have good sloping shoulders, a small head and a good crest, not ewe-necked. Good strong hind quarters, with his hocks well under him. These are only a few of the characteristics necessary to make up the perfect pony, but if your prospective purchase has them you can be reasonably sure of buying a pony which will not be difficult to balance and, therefore, will give you a fair ride.

Buying a pony with a big ugly head, straight shoulders and a weak ewe-neck, is a waste of time, as he will never give you a good ride, however much time you spend on schooling him.

Finally, I would give this advice to all young people. Do not buy your own pony until you can ride reasonably well. The only way you can learn the art of riding is by "having a go" on all different types.

If you are a complete novice, and you purchase a very quiet pony, you may find that in a year or two, when you have gained more experience, your pony has become too quiet and it will no longer be fun to ride him, as it was at first.

Jenny Younghusband

CHAPTER TWO

Looking After a Pony

JENNIFER AND DORIAN WILLIAMS

THE FIELD · FENCING · SHELTER · FEEDING · WATERING ·
THE PONY AT WORK · THE PONY LIVING IN · OUT AT GRASS ·
REGULAR SUPERVISION

*If the pony is going to remain healthy and sound and give his owner all the
pleasure of which he is capable, proper care of a pony is obviously absolutely
essential. Although ponies are strong and hardy by nature, all sorts of things can
go wrong with them unless they are properly looked after. This chapter deals
with a few simple rules, a few necessary do's and don'ts, for children who keep
a pony of their own.* Editors

IT IS POSSIBLE, of course, for the native types of ponies which are naturally strong and healthy to stay out in a field all the year round; as long as the field has proper shelter, good grass and plenty of water and as long as the pony gets plenty of food in the winter months. The more blood type of pony (that is, thoroughbred or near thoroughbred) is not so hardy, however, and it does better if kept in a stable at night during the second half of the winter. A pony should look well and happy the whole year round when given the proper attention.

Let us deal first with the pony living out.

The most Suitable Field for a Pony

No pony should be kept in a field smaller than one acre. Two acres is the ideal size and, if possible, it should be divided into two parts (or three parts if it is, say, four acres). This has a number of advantages. In the first place horses are very wasteful when grazing: they prefer the best grass and much is wasted by their walking about. Also, by walking about, they are soiling the ground. This, of course, can be overcome by grazing a few cattle or sheep in the same field; they will eat the coarser grass so that there is no waste. It is also a good idea to harrow the field, so that the dung can be well spread.

The second advantage of dividing the field is that part of it is left fresh; the pony can then always change to new, fresh pasture. Thirdly, and this can be very useful, it enables you to get a hay crop off part of your field round about May or June; this is a great help because you will need the hay in the winter and nowadays hay is very expensive.

Protection   The ideal field has plenty of protection for the pony, from both the bad weather and the hot sun. It is best, perhaps, if your field can be on a southerly slope with a good hedge to act as a shelter from the cold north-easterly wind and a few nice trees for the pony to stand under in the summer to escape the sun and the flies.

Fencing   It is essential for the field to have a good, safe fence. Posts and rails are the best: then strong, plain wire. Barbed wire can often cause accidents, and sheep-hurdles are really not strong enough. If the fence is of wire, the lower strand must not be less than one foot off the ground; the tighter the wire the safer the fence.

Shelter   A good shed is an excellent idea for the pony out all the year round, although ponies will not always use it, even in winter. They are more likely to use it in summer, to escape from the flies. They can be encouraged to use the shed by being fed there. In winter the shed can be deep-littered and a bar or a half-door put across the opening, so that the pony is kept in.

Worming

All ponies should be wormed twice a year as a precautionary measure. Worming is very easy nowadays: your local "vet"—he always and understandably prefers to be called a veterinary surgeon—will let you have a powder and, of course, the necessary information about giving it.

Feeding a Pony out at Grass

It is almost certain that a pony out at grass will need feeding during the winter. Too many people start this winter feeding too late. Obviously it depends on the condition of the pony, the condition of the field and the weather; but it is probably safe to say that a pony should start having hay during the last two months before Christmas. Often people wait until the pony begins to lose weight; but then it is almost impossible to get him to regain it. Ponies vary, of course, in the amount that they need, so the best rule is to give him as much as he will eat.

Hay-nets   The hay should be fed to the pony loose on the ground, unless you are lucky enough to have a good hay-rack. It is possible to use hay-nets, too; but they have their disadvantages as well as their advantages. They must be fixed sufficiently high off the ground for you to be sure that when they are empty the pony cannot get his foot in one. For young stock it is definitely unwise to use hay-nets because they are inclined to paw the ground and can easily get caught. On the other hand, a hay-net is more economical as it means less waste. The hay cannot get soiled or trodden on, and as the pony has to eat more slowly it is better for his digestion.

Hard foods A native pony that starts the winter looking well should easily go right through just on hay; but a pony that is going to be worked really hard or even hunted out of the field will need a little corn, bran and chaff if it is going to keep its condition.

If a pony begins to go downhill a little in a long, hard winter, a small feed in the evenings is a great help. Ponies, like children, will always be warm and happy if they are given plenty of food.

Water There is nothing more important than a good and constant supply of water in a field. A pony must be able to help himself when he wants it. A pond or stream is all right, as long as it is reasonably clean and easy for the pony to use. A stream is better than a pond because the water is likely to be cleaner and there is probably a solid bottom. Too much sand in a stream can be dangerous: if a pony swallows it he can get colic.

A tank is more usual and, if possible, it should be placed where it can easily be inspected or re-filled. It should also have a ball-cock and it

ought to be cleaned out at least twice a year.

It is really essential to remember to see that a pony has plenty of water and, of course, in winter to break the ice if necessary.

Bringing a Pony in at Night

The more blood type of pony will definitely keep fitter and better if brought in to a warm stable at night during the latter half of the winter. After Christmas the ground can get so wet or so cold that a pony will never

HAY-NET *This picture shows the right height to hang a net. Remember that it will drop as much as a foot when it is empty*

CHART FOR FEEDING

	Pony under 13 hands			Pony over 13 hands		
Part-stabled, or living out *in winter*; *in work* for hacking or hunting	*Morning* 1 lb. oats *Noon* 1 lb. oats (not necessary for a pony under 12 hands) *Night* 1 to 2 lbs. oats	1 lb. bran & chaff in each feed	Hay-net — Hay-net	*Morning* 1 lb. oats *Noon* 1 lb. oats *Night* 2 to 3 lbs. oats	1½ lbs. bran & chaff in each feed	Hay-net — Hay-net
Part-stabled, or living out *in winter*; *not in work*	*Morning* *Noon* — *Night* 1 to 2 lbs. oats with 1 lb. bran and chaff	 — 	Hay-net Hay-net	*Morning* 1 lb. oats with 1 lb. bran and chaff (not necessary for hardy type of pony) *Noon* — *Night* 1 to 2 lbs. oats with 1 lb. bran and chaff		Hay-net — Hay-net
Living out, *in summer*; *in work*	For ordinary hacking no corn is necessary, but if going to a gymkhana, or show, or Pony Club rally—especially if pony is long out of stable—it is wise to give a pony 2 to 3 lbs. of oats with 1 lb. of bran and chaff (3 to 4 lbs. for larger ponies) after work					
Living out, *in summer*; *not in work*	There is no need to give a pony any extra feed as long as there is *plenty of grass*. Should the pony be standing in in the day time to avoid flies, he will need hay. But one must watch to see that a pony does not get too fat. It will then be best to bring him in without giving him hay					

have a chance to lie down. and there will be no goodness in the grass.

It is difficult to say exactly when a pony should come in because it must depend largely on the weather. Probably the beginning of December is best. The pony should be brought in just before dark and put in the stable on a good bed of straw, with some hay, water and a small feed. There must be plenty of fresh air, too, but not a draught. Ideally the stable should face south and have a half-door.

The Pony at Work

If you are taking your pony hunting, or going to a pony club rally, it will be best if you plan a definite routine for yourself.

If he is living out he may well be wet or muddy, so you must get up early to give yourself plenty of time to clean him properly. The tack will have, or should have, been done the day before. Perhaps too he will have had a small feed overnight as a treat to prepare him for the next day. The mud must be brushed off with a dandy brush, and his mane and tail done with a body brush. Don't forget to sponge out his eyes, nose and dock. It must be remembered, however, that the grease in his coat helps to keep him warm and to protect him from wet, so the pony living out must only be dandy-brushed and not have the grease removed. A rough pony, with a long coat, can still look smart and well turned-out, so it is worth taking just that little extra trouble before you start.

Returning to stable As soon as you get home, rub your pony all over with straw to get the worst of the mud off him, feel his legs for any thorns or pricks or cuts, look at his feet in case he has picked up anything that might make him go lame, and then turn him straight out in the field, even if he is still sweating. Out in the field you can water him, give him his hay and (as long as there are not other ponies in the field to eat his feed!) feed him.

Look at him again very carefully the next day to see that he is not suffering any ill-effects.

The pony living in The pony living in needs just the same treatment as the pony living out, except that he can be more thoroughly groomed and can have a tail bandage put on first thing in the morning.

On arriving home he must be rubbed down with dry straw, given some *chilled* water and then his feed.

After you have had your own tea and before going to bed dandy-brush him as clean as possible, fill up his water bucket, and give him more hay.

It is not easy to get a pony's legs really dry after a day's hunting, but a good deep bed of straw will soon help to dry him off.

Out at Grass in the Summer

As soon as the nights are getting warmer and the good summer grass is beginning to grow, it is quite safe to let any pony stay out all night. This is usually about the middle of April. Lots of people bring their ponies in during the middle of the *day* in summer, as this prevents the ponies getting too fat when the grass is at its most lush, and also protects them from the heat of the day and the persistent, irritating flies.

Regular inspection Because a pony is out at grass it does not mean that it should be ignored. In fact it should be visited *every day*, to make sure that nothing has happened to it such as being caught up in the fence or kicked by another pony; to make sure that it is not short of water; to make sure that its feet are all right (they are so often neglected); and also to help keep it easy to catch and friendly. If a pony is just put out at grass and ignored it is not surprising if it becomes a little wild and unfriendly and then, of course, it is difficult to catch.

CHAPTER THREE

Simple Stable Management

JENNIFER WILLIAMS

THE STABLE · DOOR, WINDOW, DRAINS, FLOOR · LOOKING
AFTER THE STABLE · BEDDING · FORAGE · GROOMING ·
TACK · CLOTHING

In our opinion this is really the most important chapter in the whole book, because success with ponies can depend entirely upon stable management. If your stable management is correct this will not only make your pony happier, quieter, easier to handle and better-looking, but he will also live much longer and retain his value.

You may feel that there are rather a lot of do's and don'ts in this chapter, but in stable-management there must be rules, and they are, of course, based on hundreds and hundreds of years of experience. They are based, too, on our own practical experience of running stables and looking after ponies and horses; although we know it all means hard work we believe that it is absolutely necessary and really worthwhile.

One must always remember that a pony cannot speak. He cannot tell you his wants, or confide in you that he is tired, or cold, or not feeling very well; so it is the duty of anyone who looks after ponies to leave nothing to chance. You are then being as sure as one possibly can be that your pony is being looked after in the best possible way. If you are sure of that, then you can feel that you have a clear conscience and you can go off and enjoy yourself. But the pony must come first, because he cannot shout after you if you have forgotten something, left the door open or not mucked him out.

This chapter is rather long, so we have divided it into six sections each of which is important for you to read if you are ever lucky enough to have anything to do with a pony living in, either at home or in a riding school or livery stables where, perhaps, you sometimes lend a hand.

If you only have a pony living out, obviously the chapter on "Looking after a Pony" will be more important, but sooner or later you are sure to have a pony or horse that is in a stable for at least part of the time. Editors

The Stable

IT IS FAR more healthy for a pony if he can be given a well-ventilated and well-drained stable. Of course the ideal stable can be expensive to put up, but if you remember the main points then it is not too difficult to give your pony all that he requires. A stable should measure 12 × 10 feet and 10 feet high; a stall, 6 × 11 feet. Good ventilation and a stable free from draughts is what one most wants to aim at. The stable should be constructed on a dry foundation and away from prevailing winds; south is the best way to face as it will then get the most sunshine. The door should be divided into two halves and open outwards.

The window The window should be on the same side as the door to prevent draughts—the ideal window is called a Sherringham and it allows the air to flow inwards and then upwards, so the pony gets no cold air on his back.

The manger The manger is best put in one corner, opposite the door and there should be a ring on the same opposite wall for the hay-net.

The drains The drains are *very* important; on no condition must they be on the side where the food goes. In the best built stables the floor will slant towards the door and the drain will be on the door side.

The floor There are several kinds of floors one can have put down; the best, of course, is made of good stable brick; but this is expensive. Concrete is the most common, but it must be properly grooved to stop the pony slipping too much, and to encourage the water into the drains; chalk is also good and very economical. All the door catches should be put on in such a way that the pony cannot hurt himself (or open the door!) and the light switches must be on the outside wall.

The roof The roof is best done with slate and tiles. Corrugated iron can be very hot in summer and straw or thatch, though attractive to look at, is dangerous because it can catch fire.

The walls The walls, if brick, must be lined half way up inside with wood, otherwise they can be very rough for the pony.

Have a good light stable. Ponies like it better and a very dark stable is not good for their eyes. When constructing a stable yard it is worth remembering the following points as they will save you a lot of trouble:

Have all boxes together as ponies like company.

Have the forage and tack rooms near the stable.

Have the stable near the house and see there is easy access to hot and cold water, and somewhere to make up boiled feeds.

There are excellent portable boxes on the market now. These are made entirely of wood and have proved very satisfactory.

Looking after the Stable

To lay a bed properly and keep your stable tidy you must have the following utensils, shown below:

A two- or four-pronged fork
A barrow and a skep (basket needed for picking droppings up in)

A brush
A shovel

Bedding Why must a horse or pony have bedding? The reasons are fairly obvious: to prevent him hurting himself, to keep him warm, to absorb the water, and to help keep him clean. Wheat straw is generally used; barley

DAY BED *The correct way to put a day bed down. Notice the straw well banked up at sides*

Straw well banked up round manger in day bed

NIGHT BED *The bedding in the centre of the box should be twice as thick as the day bed*

24

is too prickly, and oat straw the pony will often eat. Other very adequate beddings include peat, sawdust (wood shavings) and bracken. Peat and saw-dust are often used to stop the animal insisting on eating his bedding; they do have their great disadvantages, however, unless every single wet patch is removed *regularly*, for otherwise the bedding becomes overheated, and the animal is liable to get what is called thrush in the frog part of the foot; sawdust can also get maggoty.

Forage

Before we start to describe the good and bad points of the various foods here are a few general principles to remember when feeding, dealing first with a pony that is stabled:

Feed little and often (a horse has a surprisingly small stomach).

Feed according to the work and condition of the animal.

Water before food; the reverse can cause colic.

All food must be clean and free from dust.

Do not work a pony too soon after feeding.

Try to give a good balanced diet with lots of bulk (hay) and always a few succulent foods (to replace the grass) such as carrots, man-golds, linseed and even treacle, because this will help to give the pony a good appetite.

Now for some details about the feeding stuffs.

Hay Hay is the most important food in a pony's diet. Good hay can be recognized in several ways: the sweet smell, the colour (which should be greenish to brownish), the look—not too weathered, no mouldy patches, and not too dusty. Hay is at its best when between six to eighteen months old, and you should, if possible, use hay from the previous year. Nowadays good hay can be so difficult to buy that it is often almost impossible to get any but the present year's hay. The older hay can be recognised by its slightly darker colour and the fact that it is more brittle—be careful that it is not just the rain that has darkened it. A second cut of hay does not usually have nearly so much goodness. Most ponies love clover hay, but it is very fattening and should not on any account be fed to animals in work. It is usually very dusty. A good mixture of clover and meadow hay is often fed. Good meadow hay is the best; it should contain all the best grasses, such as meadow, foxtail, timothy, crested, dogstail and many others. Dusty hay is very bad to feed, especially if a pony is coughing at all. If, however, he has to be given some because there is no other, shake it well before feeding and sprinkle it with water.

Oats Oats can either be black or

25

OATS AND BRAN   *The pile of oats on the right weighs* 2 lbs: *the bran on the left,* 1½ lbs. *Each would fill a normal-sized dipper and you can see how the amounts compare with an ordinary-sized stable bucket*

white; both are good. They must be dry, short and plump in appearance. Here again new oats are not so good, and the best are between nine months and two years old. The best new oats can be distinguished by their earthy smell, while old oats have hardly any smell at all. Bruised or crushed oats are really better than whole oats, because they are more easily digested.

Chaff   Chaff is excellent as a bulk food—to feed with oats if feeding a pony in the field or stable. Chaff is sliced hay and you can also add a small proportion of oat straw (two parts hay to one part oat straw).

Wheat and barley   Wheat is no good for feeding. Barley can be fed only in very small quantities and should always be boiled first and it can then help to put weight on a pony.

Bran   Bran, of course, is an excellent bulk food; it also helps put on weight. If used wet it is a laxative food and it can be mixed with oats and chaff.

It is a good idea to feed various other foods with everyday oats, but the danger then is that if one keeps adding nice little titbits, such as apples, carrots, or treacle it may tend to make the pony a fussy feeder.

Cubes   We have found that the new cubes, now manufactured by Spillers, are very effective. They are clean, easy to feed and ensure that a pony gets the proper vitamins. They are particularly useful for ponies out at grass as there is no waste. The hay consumption is considerably cut down and, of course, no oats are necessary if you are using cubes.

Watering   The stabled pony does need very careful watering and there are certain points which should always be borne in mind:

There must always be *plenty* of clean water.

It is best to water *before feeding*.

It is unwise to work fast immediately after a long drink.

A very hot pony must never be given cold water to drink; it should always have *chilled* water.

Grooming

Complete grooming kit consists of:
A dandy brush

26

A body brush
A water brush
A curry comb
A wisp
Sponge
A rubber
Combs (Mane and tail)
A hoof pick
Neat's-foot oil

Reasons for grooming Firstly, you can really alter the appearance of a pony if he is properly turned out, clean, with trimmed heels, pulled mane and tail. Secondly, it is better for the pony because it keeps him in healthier condition and free from disease.

Technique When grooming, start at the neck, then do one side and then

GROOMING KIT II *a) neat's-foot oil, b) sponge (for eyes, nose, dock), c) rubber, d) mane comb, e) hoof-pick, f) tail comb*

GROOMING KIT I *a) wisp, b) dandy brush, c) water brush, d) body brush, e) rubber curry comb, f) curry comb*

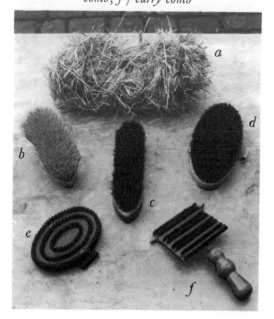

the other, leaving the pony's head until last of all. First use the dandy brush for removing mud and sweat; then the body brush with curry comb to clean it; wisp; sponge eyes, nose, dock; and finally use the rubber for the final polish.

Tack

   Equipment Two sponges (water sponge: soap sponge)
      Shammy leather
      Metal polish
      Duster
      Bucket of warm water (not hot)
      Soap

TACK CLEANING KIT *a) water sponge, b) metal polish, c) duster for polishing, d) soap sponge, e) saddle soap, f) shammy leather*

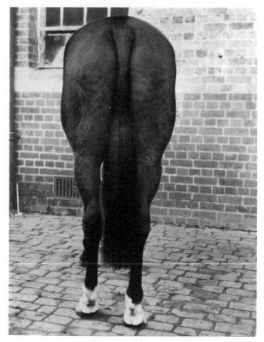

A well-pulled tail

A tail that has not been pulled

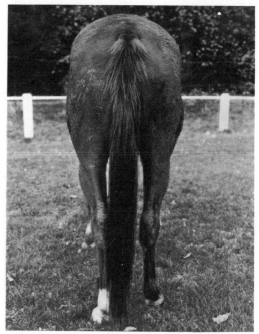

The tack must be cleaned every time that it has been used: make sure particularly that the bit is cleaned after every use.

The tack should be completely taken to pieces and cleaned at least twice each week, otherwise the leather round the buckles will become very hard.

Method of cleaning Take a bucket of warm water; wash all the dirt off with the water sponge: rub over with the shammy to remove all surplus water: soap thoroughly. Do not put the soap on so that it lathers, as this does the leather no good and will not help to soften it but will fill the holes up with soap. The soap sponge should be very thoroughly squeezed before using. It is best to polish all buckles, stirrups and bits but not the part of the bit which goes into the mouth. The leather should be soft and pliable

28

but do not let it become sticky with soap; if kept in good condition it will last much longer and, of course, it is more comfortable for the pony to wear.

Fitting of tack It is important to see that your harness *fits* properly; so often one sees a pony with a sore back which is only due to an ill-fitting saddle.

must not be too narrow, or it might pinch the pony's back. If your pony hasn't been ridden for some time and is unfit, use a nylon girth, as leather girths are so apt to cause girth galls.

Bridle The bit must be comfortable in the mouth, not wrinkling the corners Nor should it be so low that it encourages the pony to put his tongue over it. With the nose band,

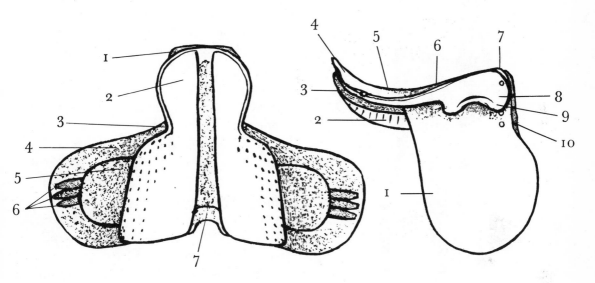

SADDLE I

1	Cantle
2	Lining
3	Waist
4	Saddle Flap
5	Sweat Flap
6	Girth Straps
7	Gullet

SADDLE II

1	Saddle flap	7	Pommel
2	Lining	8	Bars (underneath Skirts)
3	Panel		
4	Cantle	9	Skirt
5	Seat	10	Panel
6	Waist		

Saddle The front should be well off the pony and you should be able to see daylight along the gutter which is formed by the two pads on the under-neath side of the saddle. The gutter

allow the width of two fingers between the nose and the front, for tightness; and two from the side cheekbone for height of nose band. There should be room for the width of four fingers

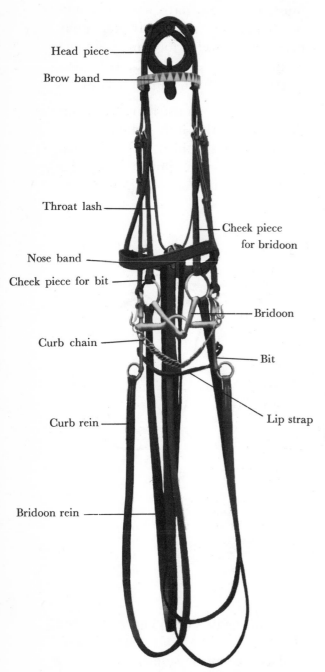

Head piece

Brow band

Throat lash

Nose band

Cheek piece for bit

Curb chain

Curb rein

Bridoon rein

Cheek piece
for bridoon

Bridoon

Bit

Lip strap

THE CORRECT WAY TO HANG UP A
DOUBLE BRIDLE

under the throat lash, as plenty of room is essential for the pony to bend his neck and head properly.

Clothing

Bandages For a pony living out, or part stabled, it is very useful to have a good tail bandage which is bound round the top of the tail to keep it neat, a set of woollen and crepe (or stockinette) bandages, a summer sheet, possibly a night or day rug, and a New Zealand rug.

Ponies living out in winter should not have pulled tails because of the cold, so there is no need for a bandage: but in summer they can wear one; the stabled pony however, can have his tail pulled and then he should wear one. The real point of using a tail bandage is to improve the shape of the tail, and to protect it when travelling. When putting a tail bandage on, first wet the tail only; start bandaging at the top; then work to the bottom of the dock and one third of the way up again. Remember to tie the tapes flat on top and not tight; tight bandaging can stop the circulation.

Woollen or stable bandages are useful for protecting legs when travelling; they keep the pony's legs warm in the stable and will help to dry the legs. Sometimes it is a good idea to use straw underneath.

Points to remember:

1) Woollen bandages: bandage

from under knee or hock right to the coronet; but do not bandage too tightly, just tight enough to make the bandage stay up properly.

2) Crepe or stockinette bandages: these can be used for exercising; the reason for these is to support the leg if there is any tendency to weakness. They must be put on fairly tight to give good support, but you should only bandage as far down as the top of the fetlock joint; whatever happens the movement of the joint must not be hampered.

3) All tapes must be tied flat, either inside or outside; tie them in a bow and tuck ends in.

4) Make sure the bandage has been rolled the right way up so that the tape end is lying perfectly flat.

Rugs A night rug can be useful when the pony has a chill and must be kept warm; on occasions the stabled pony may need one, especially if he has been partly clipped out in winter. Night rugs are made of jute and lined with woollen blanket.

Summer sheets or day rugs are very nice to own, as perhaps sometimes during the summer at a pony club rally or gymkhana they can be very useful, either to keep your pony dry or protect him from the flies.

New Zealand rugs are most popular nowadays for ponies trace-clipped and stabled. When the weather is really

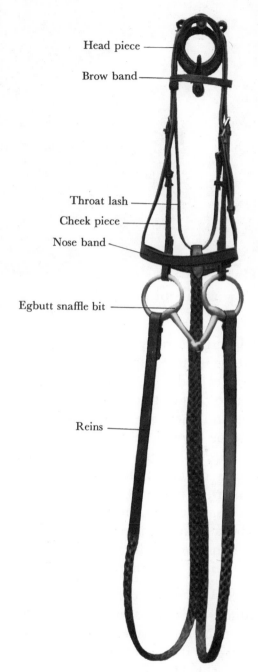

Head piece

Brow band

Throat lash

Cheek piece

Nose band

Egbutt snaffle bit

Reins

THE CORRECT WAY TO HANG UP A SNAFFLE BRIDLE

31

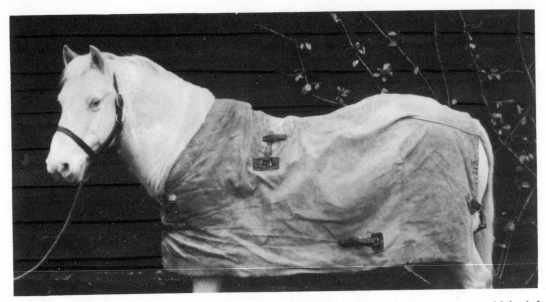

A NEW ZEALAND RUG *This picture shows a good-fitting rug, in which a pony could be left out in winter without any worry*

cold and the pony has to go in the field, he is quite safe turned loose in a New Zealand rug. These cannot slip, because of the straps round the hind legs, and they are waterproof; one must be careful, however, that the rug does not make him sore on the withers or chest, as there is continual rubbing.

Rugs, of course, must have rollers or belts to keep them in place. They can either match the rug, or they can be obtained in leather.

Halters Halters can be rope or leather. It is important when tying your pony up to remember to see that the rope is the right length; when too short it holds the pony's head too tight, when too long it enables the pony to get caught up in it.

It is essential to tie the knot correctly.

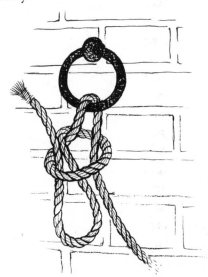

HALTER *The right way to tie the knot so that the pony cannot pull it loose, but should the pony run back it is very quick to release it by pulling the spare end*

Jennifer Williams

CHAPTER FOUR

Simple Schooling

JENNIFER AND DORIAN WILLIAMS

PATIENCE · TITBITS · TYING UP · THE MOUTH · OBEDIENCE ·
SEAT · LEGS · HANDS · AIDS · THE VOICE · WALK · TROT ·
CANTER · HALT · REIN BACK · TEMPERAMENT · *CAVALETTI* ·
SIMPLE JUMPING · A LANE · PARALLEL POLES · DOUBLES AND
TREBLES · IMPULSION · COMPETITIONS · SEAT AND HANDS FOR
JUMPING · BALANCE

It always seems that people who have horses and ponies either think that schooling of any sort is quite unnecessary, or think that it is only possible to get proper schooling (of the horse or pony and the rider) from an expert, probably at considerable cost.

Schooling, of course, is absolutely necessary; but if you follow carefully the advice of those who have had a good deal of experience it is really possible to carry out much of the instruction and schooling yourself. In many ways this is more fun than letting someone else do it all. Anyway, practising yourself can supplement the schooling and instruction that you can get, from time to time, from a school.

There is no doubt at all that the better you ride and the better your pony is schooled the more pleasure you will get.   Editors

The Pony

SCHOOLING A PONY requires great patience, but patience, although very important, is by no means the only thing needed, for ponies can be very cunning and naughty. Far too many ponies are allowed to have their own way and this (as in the case of children!) does not necessarily do them good or make them happy. Teaching a pony anything, however simple, requires an understanding between pony and child: but what is most important is that the pony should have *respect* for his owner. Patience, understanding, and respect from the animal, form the real basis

33

CORRECT METHOD OF PICKING UP
FOOT *Notice position of hands and how the
back is kept towards the pony's head*

*The foot correctly held, the weight in the right
hand, leaving the left hand free to use pick if
necessary*

for all schooling, however simple or advanced. A pony that is obedient, well-mannered and a pleasure to handle is obviously the nicer kind of pony to own; as a rule ponies are only like that because of the way they have been treated; if a rider is nervous, irritable or bad tempered, you will find that it soon shows on the pony; just as it will show if the owner is patient, placid and good-tempered.

Titbits Ponies are often given titbits: but these do tend to make a pony so very nippy, that it really is advisable to limit them, so that the pony is not always expecting something to eat whenever you go near him.

Standing still Teach your pony, when you first get him, to stand still when you mount. This is one of the first lessons in obedience, and it is such a help, especially if it is rather a long way up. When you get on, do not let him walk off until you are quite ready, having gathered up your reins properly and got both feet firmly in the stirrups; then tell him to walk on. There is nothing more annoying than to own a pony which hates standing still, even for a minute.

CORRECT METHOD OF MOUNTING *By having her back towards the head the rider will be propelled towards the saddle if the pony moves forward*

THE INCORRECT METHOD OF MOUNTING *The rider has no control of the pony, and if he does move forward she will sit down hard and might even hurt the back of her head*

Tying up It can be so very useful if your pony is easy to tie up in the yard, especially at pony club rallies and gymkhanas. Get him into the habit of being tied up every day for a short time, while he is being groomed, or when you are busy in the stables. Remember, though, to tie him up with a *slip knot*, so that if something frightens him and he starts pulling back you are able to release him quickly. Nothing puts a pony off being tied up more than if he has run back and broken a halter.

The mouth A pony with a good mouth is a joy to ride. The trouble is that so many ponies are badly broken in, so that by the time you get them their mouths have been ruined. Nothing will harm a pony's mouth quicker than a severe bit and a rider with hard hands. A mouth can, of course, be greatly improved by the soft, sensitive hands of a good rider and the proper use of the rider's legs and seat. A well-balanced ride is mainly due to the pony's conformation, but to be well-balanced a pony does not necessarily have to have good conformation.

35

Obedience A most important thing is to make your pony obedient so that you can make him go exactly where you want, when you want. The worst thing for a pony is to do the same things every day: always to go out with others, always go round in a circle, always following another pony. So often then, when you want to turn and go somewhere else, the pony gets stubborn and neighs and fidgets. Try to mix the work that you give your pony. Sometimes, when out for a ride, make your pony turn and canter away from the others and then back again. If he is difficult, remember to be *firm* and *patient*. It is always much more fun if your pony has an interesting ride, so whatever you do, do not always ride him round and round the same field, or he will quickly become bored with life. Variety is much the best thing to keep him really interested in going *forward*, which, after all, is what you want him to do. In more technical terms this is called "free forward movement". Until your pony has acquired it, it is impossible to teach him anything very advanced. Once he really goes forward when you want him to you have gained a great deal, for he can then learn to be obedient to the pressure of your legs and hands.

All this will help your pony to be far more enjoyable to ride. Then if you wish him to do more advanced things in the pony club and at

shows you are on the right road to do so.

The Rider

When one is lucky enough to start riding it is advisable to learn the basic things right at the beginning, such as the correct use of hands, seat and legs. It is most important to get complete confidence and to have practical experience; too much instruction, especially if it comes from several different people, can be very confusing and gives the pupil no chance to mould his or her own style of riding. This is especially so with young children. Children under ten do not want instruction for more than an hour at a time, and that not too often; they will gain far more if they have the opportunity to ride a nice, narrow, kind, willing pony and are allowed to get on and do things by themselves. A rider with lots of confidence and "go" will learn the educated side of horsemanship very quickly.

First of all, then, let us deal with the correct position of seat, hands and legs. The aim is to try to cultivate an entirely independent, firm seat, so as not to depend on the reins for support. Everything in riding is the combination of hands and legs, and until an independent strong position is formed it is impossible to learn very much. The weight of your body should remain in the centre of the saddle. When getting on the pony, make sure you are in the correct position by first taking your feet out of the stirrups, relaxing, then wriggling your seat into the centre of the saddle; take the stirrups up again, making sure they are the right length (the test, for riding with an all-purpose length, is that when sitting on the pony with relaxed legs, the bottoms of the stirrups should come to your ankle bones). You should sit well down in the saddle with a good straight back. Try not to stiffen any part of the body as this can cause difficulties.

The knees and thighs   One grips with

Quite a nice seat but a little too stiff, with the seat pushed outwards instead of into the saddle and the forearms and wrists a little too rigid

THE CORRECT SEAT   *A nice, relaxed position that gives the appearance of being easy and natural*

these—not the calf; remember to grip downwards and inwards and not upwards.

The toes should be kept up above the level of the heels; press well down with the heels as this helps you to grip on the *inside* of the thigh and knee and also to grip down and not up. The toe should be just in front of a perpendicular line down from the knee; in fact, if the stirrup leather is hanging straight down the bottom half of the leg, the leg-position is correct.

The arms   They should hang naturally to the elbows, which should

37

lightly touch the body; the hands should be just in front of the pommel of the saddle, with wrists and fingers quite supple, thumbs facing upwards and slightly inwards; but be careful not to round your wrists. Good hands are supple and sensitive, as is the whole body of a good rider. Do not look down; your head should be erect. To help you to obtain this good seat position there is nothing better than riding without stirrups, as this forces you right down into the saddle and strengthens the grip. There are, of course, many exercises to give a little variety, such as touching your toes and bending right forward, and then back until your head touches the pony's rump. For exercises like this you must have a pony which does not object to such treatment. Most will soon become accustomed to it.

The next step, once the position is correct, is to know the *aids*.

The aids There are two groups of aids:

1) The natural ones, through which the rider conveys his intentions to the horse or pony and which they must learn to understand and obey. These are the hands, legs, body and voice.

2) The "artificial aids", such as whips, spurs, martingales—a leather strap attached to the girth and back of noseband ("standing martingale") or reins ("running mar-

tingale") and used to hold a pony's head down, gags, etc.

Two of these aids, the whip and voice, are very useful for the preliminary training on a young horse so that through them he can eventually learn to understand the natural aids. All the artificial aids must be used with intelligence, as some of them can be extremely unkind to a horse.

Before we give you the aids for the walk, trot and canter let us first see what part the natural aids play in controlling the horse.

The legs They help to guide and control the hindquarters; also they create impulsion and energy.

The hands In conjunction with the legs they regulate the energy created by the legs, help to control the forehand and also guide and control the pace.

The body Very important. By its distribution of weight, forward, backward or sideways, it helps the animal to carry out what is being asked of him. The weight of the body should always be going very slightly in the direction of the movement. (The exception to this rule is a movement called "shoulder-in", which we are not dealing with here as it is more advanced.)

The voice This is a great asset, especially in teaching a young pony

LEGS *A nice, firm position with the knee well rolled into the saddle so that the rider is gripping with the thigh, and not the calf*

The legs are too far back, the heel not down, so that the balance is wrong and there is no proper grip

and also, used the right way, to quieten a frightened or nervous pony. A firm voice is extremely important when handling a pony on the ground.

Walk Shorten up your reins to the correct length; squeeze with both legs, then drive forward with seat and legs. When the pony moves forward relax pressure with legs, and feel the reins so as to maintain the pace required.

Trot If going from a walk, remember first to shorten up your reins and then use the same aids as for walking. To go into a strong trot, use more pres-

sure with legs; the horse will want to use slightly more neck, but it is very important still to maintain the same feel on the reins.

Canter If using the diagonal aids (the use of the left leg or hand to move the pony to the right or *vice versa*) the simplest way is: first the rider should cease trotting and sit down in the saddle; then use the outside leg behind the girth, and the inside one very slightly on the girth; the weight of the body also shifts slightly on the outside seat bone. On no account must you look down to see onto which

HANDS: THE SNAFFLE *The right way to hold a snaffle: at slow paces it is also correct to have the rein between the third and little fingers*

leg the pony has struck; you must learn to feel which foreleg is leading.

Aids to halt Use both legs, resist with hands and bring the weight of the body slightly back; this will help drive the pony up to his bit, so that he halts with a still head and his weight evenly distributed over all four legs. Immediately the pony halts relax the leg pressure and the feel on the reins.

Rein back Make a good square halt with the pony well between the legs and hands. Make him step back with

an even rhythm; a slight pressure of legs at first, until you feel him about to move, then relax the pressure, but maintain the feel on the reins to make your pony move the required number of steps backwards; then relax the feel on the reins and squeeze him forward.

Many ponies are difficult to rein back and this is very often due to physical difficulties, such as stiffness. It is a waste of time to force a pony to rein back if he is too stiff. To make him supple you will have to give him a lot of hard, concentrated work to teach him to accept the bit and learn to be really obedient to your hands and legs.

This will mean much patience; but all schooling demands patience if it is to be effective.

Jumping

For many children their greatest ambition is to *jump*. In fact it is far easier to learn to jump than to learn what we call educated horsemanship: that is, the ability to school a horse properly, so that it can carry out a dressage test really well.

Temperament of the pony As you will very quickly discover, ponies are either so lazy that they do not seem to want to jump at all, or else they are so impetuous that they want to fly at a fence the moment they see it. For either type of pony these simple suggestions will be effective. In the case of the former they will wake the pony up and get him supple and obedient; in the case of the latter they will steady him—that is very important indeed, because with impetuous ponies (generally the better bred type) jumping goes to their heads, like alcohol with human beings! They get over excited and then they cannot jump properly. Usually the more they jump the more excited they get, which is why at shows, even the big ones, you often see ponies which cannot be properly controlled, and therefore have to have severe bridles. But

if a pony is properly schooled from the beginning he will be steady.

Cavaletti It is best to start by taking your pony over the lowest possible pole. Take him over it first of all at a walk, then a trot; take him in both directions, and always very steadily.

The ideal poles for this simple training are called *cavaletti*. They are about six or seven feet long and stand on little crossed ends which by being turned round can vary the height, and are so constructed as to make it difficult for the poles to fall. If you have no *cavaletti*, or means to make

THE DOUBLE BRIDLE *The right way to hold a double bridle, just enough contact being maintained with the pony's mouth*

THE WRONG WAY *The reins are too slack and with the hands in this position the rider looks like a dog sitting up and begging*

41

CAVALETTI   *A simple pole which can vary in height from the ground according to which way up the ends are placed*

them, good logs are quite a useful substitute. The idea of these *cavaletti*, or logs, is to place them about four or five feet apart and then make your horse or pony trot over them. By doing this very simple and in your opinion, perhaps, boring exercise you are achieving three extremely useful results.

1) You are teaching your pony to lower his head and stretch it out, which is absolutely essential if he is going to jump well.

2) You are helping him to learn to be careful and accurate with his feet and to know where to put them so that he will easily be able to get over the poles. This helps to balance him.

3) You are making him *steady*, because if he hots up he just cannot go over the *cavaletti* without hitting them and getting in a muddle.

Many people start putting their ponies over *cavaletti* on the lunge (a long leather tape attached to the pony's head by a piece of harness known as a cavison), because this

A pony trotting over cavaletti

A line of cavaletti *placed about 5 ft. apart ready to be used for an exercise*

means that they do it without any interference from the rider. If somebody pulls on the pony's reins or shifts their weight in the saddle, it will easily unbalance him. Lunging him over the *cavaletti* will also make him calm.

Patience   It is, of course, of the utmost importance that you should be patient. Patience is well worth while, for if you are content to start your pony, especially if he is young, going over logs or *cavaletti* at a steady *trot*, then as soon as he starts jumping

proper fences you will find that he is balanced and controlled, and will jump much better.

Simple fences   When you are satisfied that you have achieved what you wanted with the *cavaletti*, you can put up a small brush fence, or a pole. But in neither case does it want to be too easy to knock down, because then a pony will quickly get careless. You can easily build a little brush fence, but see that it has a heavy base, which will prevent it from falling over.

If you are going to use a pole, it is

A pony cantering over cavaletti. (*To be really critical, the rider's position is not sufficiently forward*)

43

a good idea to lay another pole on the ground just in front of it. When a horse jumps he focuses on the ground line—that is, the base of the fence—and that is how he judges his stride. A single pole, therefore, if it is high, is the hardest type of fence to jump, because there is no ground line. A single pole at four feet is a much harder fence to jump than a triple bar at four feet six inches. You want to make your fences as easy-looking as possible: then your pony will enjoy jumping.

A lane What is really ideal is a narrow lane down one side of a school, where you can put up a number of little fences and make your pony go over them again and again. You can have him on the lunge and run by the side; or you can ride him, or if it is an *enclosed* school you can send him down the lane, loose, on his own. This makes him jump really freely and naturally.

Parallel poles Once you have got the pony going happily over simple fences, then bring in a second pole, so that he is jumping little parallel bars. This is a very important step indeed. By making the fence wide as well as high you are doing two things:

1) You are making him *look* and *think*, which will teach him to concentrate when jumping.

2) You are teaching him to stretch out his neck, so that he arches his back. That is what we call good style.

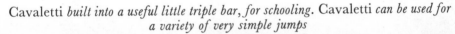

Cavaletti *built into a useful little triple bar, for schooling.* Cavaletti *can be used for a variety of very simple jumps*

JUMPING *A simple pole, which is quite enough, either for a novice pony or an inexperienced rider, for a start*
Above: *The take off. The pony finding its confidence goes well over the top*
Below: *Landing. Notice how, although the rider has been a little left behind, there is no holding on to the pony's mouth*

A LITTLE MORE ADVANCED *A young rider at a local show jumps a simple fence in almost faultless style*

Doubles and trebles The third stage in our simple training is to put the pony over a combination of fences: little doubles and trebles. It is very important that the distance between the fences should be correct, otherwise you will find that a pony gets into trouble, because he cannot reach the second part of a double; and that puts him off. You can arrange your double so that there is room either for one stride, or two strides between the two parts. For one stride, one non-jumping stride that is, you will want about twenty feet; for two strides you need about thirty feet.

Impulsion Riding over doubles you must see that you do not let your pony "creep", by which we mean, put in more strides than he should, because then he will lose all his impulsion and will not have enough "go" to make the next fence. This impulsion is very important indeed, and if you find your pony is rather sticky, then take him round and round jumping the same two or three fences again and again and again, not just three or four times, but *twenty* or *thirty* times. This will *get him going*. Jumping on a sticky pony is no fun. But this does not mean that you want to horoosh madly at the gallop, so that your pony is jumping off his forehand. He must always be collected, and should jump off his hocks. He will do this if you have:

1) Started him slowly over poles.

2) Promoted him gradually to a single fence, to be jumped *steadily*, out of a trot to begin with.

3) Introduced him, when he is ready, to parallel poles and combinations: but only when he is ready.

Competitions When you think your pony is ready to enter a competition take him along to a show where you know they will build a not too difficult course and let him get *experience*.

Do not expect him to do too well the first or second time. It will all be very strange for him, very different from home, so he will not really be concentrating. Take him round slowly, letting him have a good look at the fences. And if, by luck, you should do well and there is a jump off, have the courage to withdraw, if you feel that they are putting the fences up higher than your pony is ready to face. It is fatal to overface, or ask too much of, a pony. The reason why one sees so many ponies refusing is because they have been overfaced. And, please, the *minimum* of stick. One sharp tap is quite enough to let him know he has done wrong, if he has been properly schooled at home.

The seat One has only to watch jumping on television to realize that there are many different styles for riding over fences. This is because *balance* plays such an important part in jumping. Many children today would think it a waste of time to learn to sit properly, but there is no doubt that this gives you better balance and a better seat over fences. This, in the opinion of many experts, can only be achieved by riding *without stirrups*, and preferably without reins, while being lunged in a small circle. Thus, as it were, you fall naturally into the proper position, without being dependent upon the stirrups or the reins.

It is then comparatively easy to adjust your position for jumping, because already you are basically in the correct position.

Nowadays the "forward seat" is universally accepted for jumping (study the pictures of jumpers in this book). This means that the weight goes *forward* as you approach the fence, remains forward as the horse reaches the top of his leap, and goes down and forward with the horse as he lands. The feet should be pressed *down* against the stirrup-irons, or even slightly back, as the horse rises, to propel the weight forward.

Hands If a rider has good hands he will never hinder a horse or pony from jumping, because, as you will remember, the horse's head must be free to stretch out as it approaches the take-off. But bad hands will ruin a horse or pony.

It is not easy to describe good hands, but there should be, through the hands, a steady, sympathetic contact between horse and rider. This can only be achieved if the hands are *still*. Watch Pat Smythe or the great Italian brothers, d'Inzeo. The position of their hands hardly moves. They are maintaining contact with their mounts through the flexibility of their wrists and the suppleness of their fingers. By keeping their hands still they are keeping their horse's

heads *steady*, and this means that the horse has a better chance of seeing the fence, focusing, and judging his stride. The expert rider will lengthen his horse's stride, just by giving him a little more rein, and shorten it by a slight turn of his wrists.

The reins should *never* be used as something to hang on to. If a pony feels that his mouth is being pulled at he will soon get his head in the air. That is why so many ponies have to wear tight martingales; this is an attempt by the rider to keep their heads down. If your pony is a little impulsive and you feel that you may be "left behind" and so have to hang on to the reins, it is much better to slip your finger through the neck strap and hang on to that, otherwise it is impossible for a pony to jump freely.

There is no better exercise, if you can arrange it, than to go down a lane of jumps or round a school over the jumps with the reins knotted loose on the pony's neck, and *your arms folded*. This very quickly teaches you not to interfere with your pony's mouth. Better still, throw away your stirrups too, and then you really *will* learn how to balance yourself over jumps. You will also learn that a firm grip with the *knees*, which should be rolled into the saddle, is essential if you are not going to *lose* your balance.

Seat, hands, knees: those are the things to concentrate on if you are going to be a good rider over fences.

CHAPTER FIVE

Minor Ailments

JENNIFER WILLIAMS

THE MEDICINE CUPBOARD · FOMENTATIONS · TUBBING ·
HOSING · WOUNDS AND CUTS · ANTI-TETANUS · SADDLE SORES
AND GIRTH GALLS · CRACKED HEELS · WINDGALLS · CAPPED
HOCKS AND ELBOWS · SIDEBONES AND RINGBONES · SPRAINS ·
COLIC · A PONY IN GOOD CONDITION

Obviously, if you are in any doubt about your pony's health you must call in a veterinary surgeon, but if you take the trouble to learn a little about the simple ailments that a pony can have and how to treat them, then you will save your vet., who is probably very overworked, a lot of trouble. You will also save yourself a lot of money.

In this chapter we have dealt with the most common everyday ailments that you will encounter, sooner or later, if you have anything to do with horses and ponies. We have tried to give you a little practical advice about dealing with these troubles. But remember, if you are at all worried, get the advice and help of your vet.   Editors

*M*edicine cupboard With a pony, whether he lives in the stable or out in the field, it is an excellent idea to have a small medicine cupboard of your own consisting of a few items that are most likely to be needed. The following are suggested :

A thermometer
A pair of scissors
A bottle of disinfectant
A small bottle of iodine
A colic drench
A bottle of cough electuary

A bottle of lead lotion
Boracic powder
Antiseptic powder
A tin of Kaolin paste or a packet of Animalintex
A tin of vaseline
Two different sized calico bandages
A roll of cotton wool
Gamgee tissue (like tough cotton-wool) and lint

It will often save a visit from your veterinary surgeon if you can take the trouble to learn how to *treat* the elementary minor ailments. Firstly, it is very important to remember that hot water treatment *draws* and cold water *disperses*; so before treating any form of swelling or sprain, make quite certain which method is correct for that particular injury.

Fomentation

This is for use where there are pain and swellings, due to septic wounds, sprains and contusions.

Methods Use a clean bucket and a clean, thick white towel of medium size. Fill a bucket with warm water adding either disinfectant or salt, the latter is excellent for drawing, when there is no open wound. Fold the towel in four and hold two corners, immerse it in the bucket and then wrap it round the injured part. Repeat this for twenty minutes or so, keeping the water at the right temperature. You will probably use two bucketfuls during the time. Use water hot enough to be comfortable, remembering, though, that if there is no open wound, hotter water can be used, as it first has to penetrate through the hair. It may be necessary to repeat the fomentation three times a day in bad cases.

Tubbing

Used for the lower half of the leg, mainly for the foot.

Method Use a wooden bucket, if possible. First rub the foot scrupulously clean inside and outside. Refill the bucket with warm water at the correct temperature, and mix in some disinfectant; place the foot in the bucket for 15–20 minutes, keep one hand in the water to test temperature, which must always be kept fairly high, as tubbing with cold water is a waste of time. But, take care, very hot water could blister the leg.

Hosing

A cold stream of water running down the leg is excellent treatment if you want to clean wounds; help disperse a bruise or reduce the pain and swelling from a sprain.

Method Always start with the hose on the pony's foot and work upwards to the injury; if you do it that way he will not object. Continue for twenty minutes and repeat two or three times a day, if necessary. *Do remember to dry the heels very thoroughly* after each treatment, otherwise your pony will get cracked heels.

Wounds

There are four types of wounds which are extremely common and are, perhaps, more often experienced with ponies living out.

Clean cut These are the least common and are caused by sharp-edged objects, such as knives, razors and pieces of glass. Because of their clean surfaces they do heal quickly.

Lacerated or torn Caused by such

things as projecting nails and barbed wire. They do not usually bleed as much as clean-cut wounds.

Bruises These are caused by such things as kicks, falls, blows, or over-reaching, and are probably the most common of all.

Punctured Produced by penetrating stakes, thorns, pricks, or pointed instruments, such as nails in the feet.

Treatment Control the bleeding; if the bleeding is not bad the exposure to the air will be enough to make the blood clot over the wound. If, however, it is excessive, the blood is bright red and coming in spurts, this means a severed artery. A tourniquet is then the best remedy. To put a tourniquet on, place a flat pebble inside a handkerchief and tie on the leg between the wound and the heart. In bad cases a veterinary surgeon must be called in.

Clean throughout. This is extremely important and cannot be emphasized too strongly; cleanliness will greatly speed the healing of the wound. Wash all dirt away in warm water and a weak solution of disinfectant—Dettol is best. The hosepipe can also be used (use for 15–20 minutes). It is a good idea to clip away the hair round the cut to help keep it clean. Be extremely careful, if the cut is near a joint, not to rupture joint oil. Joint oil is a thick, sticky liquid which oozes out if the joint has been damaged and loss of it can be very serious indeed.

Protection It is advisable these days with any sort of cut, however small, especially if incurred in the hunting field or during the winter when there is much mud about, to get your veterinary surgeon to come and give an anti-tetanus injection. This must be given quite soon after your pony has been injured.

If the cut is bad and low down on the leg, it may be advisable to keep the pony in, and loosely bandage with woollen bandages, using gamgee underneath. Always allow for swelling when bandaging over an injury.

Remember that during the summer ponies may be troubled by flies: bring the pony in away from them, or make quite certain the cut is well covered with antiseptic powder. Remember, too, that if a pony is standing in he will not need any oats and is better fed on mashes and green foods. Watch the leg for swelling; it may be advisable to foment or tub it, or even put a poultice on it. Also make quite certain the cut does not need stitching as this must be done immediately.

Lesser Ailments
There are other wounds which it is advisable to know about, because they are the more usual everyday ones such as:

Saddle sores Saddle sores are caused by badly fitting saddles. The pony must be rested, of course, to treat this, and you must foment the sores, later hardening off with salt and water, or methylated spirits. It is most important, then, to get your saddle altered.

Girth galls These are usually due to a leather girth used on a fat, unfit pony. Rest the pony, and treat as for saddle sore. Make sure to use a *nylon* girth.

Bit injuries Caused by badly fitted bits, or rough hands. Wash the pony's mouth with salt and water and try changing the bit.

Cracked heels These are more often found on the pony stabled or part stabled. They are due to wet conditions and not drying the heels after washing the legs. Cracked heels can make a pony very lame. Wash the legs daily with warm water and white soap; rinse and dry very thoroughly, and then apply an ointment, which is easily obtained from your local vet.

Skin Troubles

There are many skin diseases, some contagious and some non-contagious. The contagious ones are considered the more important such as:

Mange The main symptom is intense irritation of the skin, making the pony want to scratch. Usually mange appears on neck and shoulders, the affected parts becoming thickened and wrinkled, while the hair falls off, leaving small crusts. This disease is scheduled under the Diseases of Animals Act and, if suspected, must be reported to your local authority. Luckily it is not very common.

Itchy mane and tail This can be a symptom of *worms* or a disorder of the blood condition. You will notice that the pony wants to rub himself all the time. Keep him off fresh grass and feed him on hay. Get some powder to put in the water you wash him in, and some ointment to rub on.

Ringworm This is highly contagious. The symptoms are raised circular patches of hair, usually on neck and shoulders, the hair falls off, leaving greyish white crusts. The pony should be isolated immediately. Wash the patches with a warm solution of washing soda and apply an iodine ointment.

Lice Usually found on horses in very poor condition, or on ponies out at grass. The lice can be seen on a warm day on the surface of the coat. Cure them by cleaning the pony thoroughly and applying Derris Root or D.D.T. powder.

The non-contagious skin troubles are not so common or so important. They are Humour, Nettlerash, Grease, Heel bug, Warts and others.

Lameness

This is the most common thing that can go wrong with any pony, so it is a great help to learn some of its many causes. Firstly, let us deal with the methods for testing a lame pony to discover where the lameness is.

Run the pony up, in hand, with no rider. It is a good idea to do this after he has stood still for some time.

Lame in front First, feel the legs to try to detect any heat, pain or swelling. Then get someone to trot him, first away from you, and then towards

is an excellent guide if lameness is in hocks or below; the hip is usually carried higher that side than the other. If lameness is above the hock the lame side will droop with action and the pony's body will not be carried in a straight line.

Lame in the shoulder First pull the pony's leg forward and then back-

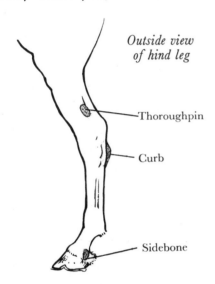

Outside view
of hind leg

Thoroughpin

Curb

Sidebone

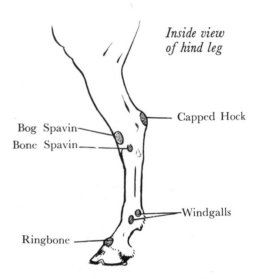

Inside view
of hind leg

Capped Hock

Bog Spavin

Bone Spavin

Windgalls

Ringbone

you, *slowly*. If lame in one foot only he will nod his head each time the *sound* leg comes to the ground. If he is lame in both legs, he will take short pottering steps.

If he is lame in the *foot*, it may be due to many things, such as a stone in the foot, bruised sole, nail binding, pricked foot, fever in the foot, etc.

Lame behind Carry out as for the front legs, but take very special notice of how level he moves his *hips*. This

wards as far as it will go. Repeat this two or three times and see if he flinches at all; then trot him immediately after, as this is an excellent test. To find if he is lame in the shoulder and not in the foot, trot the pony up and down a slight hill. If he goes more lame going uphill then suspect the shoulder; but if he is more lame coming down the hill it suggests lameness in the foot.

Splints You will not often find splints

occurring after a pony is six years old. "Splints" are bony enlargements situated on the splint bone, cannon bone or both. They are common inside front legs and are caused by too much work before the horse or pony is mature, or by blows. When splints are forming your pony may go lame, as the splint is painful to the touch. After they have formed, unless so near a joint that they interfere with the movement, they should never cause lameness.

Curb Situated on the back of the hock, three or four inches from the point of hock; the ligament, or tendon, is sprained due to overwork or sudden strain. A bow shape then appears (see diagrams). Curbs are more likely to appear on hocks that are very weak in conformation. A horse or pony with a curb must be rested. It will then probably have to have a blister or be fired. A blister caused by the application of certain ointments, preferably by the vet., strengthens the ligaments and tendons. Firing, which *must* be done by a vet., is very much more severe. It is wisest to ask a veterinary surgeon's advice.

Bone spavin Bony enlargement on the lower part of the inside of hock bone. This again is due to strain. The animal will probably go more lame on first coming out. Ask advice for treating this which is not very common.

Bog spavin A soft swelling of the hock joint on the inside and more to the front. Usually painful, it will certainly cause lameness. Treat with

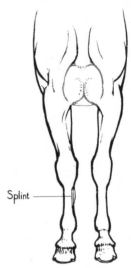

Splint

The foreleg, showing splint

hot and cold fomentations. If bad a blister may be necessary later on.

Thoroughpin A soft swelling on the upper back part of the hock which can be pushed from one side to the other. This is due to strain, and a blister will probably be necessary.

Windgalls Soft swellings above the fetlock joints on both sides. They seldom cause lameness, unless very bad. Rest the pony for a day or two if bad. Apply lead lotion bandages; or hose the legs after use.

Capped hocks and elbows Mainly due to lying down without enough bedding. If given attention when first forming and soft to feel, they can be got rid of; but not if allowed to harden. They look most unsightly, but seldom cause lameness. Treat first by cold water and massage; then, to reduce use fuller's earth and vinegar, or Radiol, or a mild blister may be necessary.

Sidebones Formed in the region of the feet causing the animal to lose some elasticity of the foot. An enlargement can be felt. Rest for a while and use cold applications; a special shoe can help.

Ringbones Found either "low" or "high"; on the coronet or above it. Enlargements of pastern bones. Due to sprains and blows but also can be inherited. A pony will be more lame on hard ground than on soft. A long rest is needed, during which a blister and special shoeing are necessary. Seek advice.

Sprains Fetlock joints become painful and swell; treat with cold water and cooling lead lotion bandages. If they are very bad first use hot fomentations and poultice to reduce inflammation, then cold water and lead lotion bandages.

Sprained tendons are also very usual—the check and suspensory ligaments become hot, painful and swollen due to sprain. If bad, remove inflammation first with hot fomentations and poulticing, then by cold hosing and soaked lead lotion bandage.

Colic

This is very similar to a stomach-ache in a human being, and can be easily recognized in a pony because he will keep walking round the stable, looking at his flanks and trying to lie down. Perhaps he will break out in a sweat and he may be straining to pass a dropping or urine; he will probably have a temperature. Colic may be due to one of the following causes: a stoppage in his stomach, too much water after a feed, bad food, such as mouldy hay or oats, or sand in drinking water.

Treatment Keep the pony warm and put a rug on him. Watch him all the time and do not let him roll, as this may cause a twisted gut. A short walk may help. Try and make him stale. Give him a colic drench. After an hour, if he is no better, call a veterinary surgeon.

To end this chapter it is perhaps fitting to remember a few points to observe when your pony is in *good* condition:

1) a bright eye
2) a good loose skin and glossy coat (the opposite means worms)
3) a bright and alert outlook
4) the pony standing squarely on *all four feet*
5) droppings the right texture
6) nostrils distended and clear.

Jennifer Williams.

CHAPTER SIX

Native Pony Breeds

MRS. I. M. YEOMANS

CONNEMARAS · DARTMOORS · DALES · EXMOORS · FELLS ·
HIGHLANDS · NEW FOREST · SHETLANDS · WELSH

It is not surprising that British ponies are famous all over the world, when you consider that we have no less than nine different breeds, each of which has a long history and a fine tradition. Each breed has its own stud-book and a pony is only recognized as a real member of its particular breed if it is in the stud-book. It is all the more interesting if you can recognize the different breeds and know something of their background, so we have asked Mrs Yeomans (a great authority) to introduce them all to you. Editors

YOUNG PEOPLE these days born into an age of fast aircraft, motor cars, motor bicycles, lorries, express trains and even long-distance push bikes, must find it very hard to realize that it is not so long ago that everyone all over the world depended on some animal, their own feet (or maybe someone else's feet!) or a boat to move them from place to place.

The British people were luckier than some in those days because there have been excellent breeds of ponies in these islands for thousands of years.

It should be realized that even wheeled vehicles are of fairly modern usage for ordinary purposes. Even kings and queens travelled on horseback together with their retinue and their goods and chattels—all on the backs of cobs and ponies. History tells us that coaches were not in general use until after the accession of James I, and then mainly in the towns where they were disliked at first!

For many hundreds of years everyone rode on the backs of smallish horses and ponies. The famous Bayeux tapestry shows horsemen—lances, shields, chain-mail and all—obviously mounted on ponies not much over fourteen hands! These must have been some of the "best" horses.

It can easily be imagined that horsemasters through the ages soon found out the best types of mount for reliability, endurance, and, in time, appearance. It is the descendants of these that are still with us today in our nine native breeds.

A CONNEMARA PONY *A really beautiful model, with a very good foreleg and sweet expression having all one could ask for in a good riding pony. Connemaras also do a lot of pack work, carrying heavy loads of peat*

In many British ponies there is Arab blood, for several infusions have been made; the Romans brought their horses with them; William the Conqueror introduced new blood including Spanish horses brought from North Africa—Arabian and barb; several private people brought over high-priced Arab horses via Italy, Turkey, etc. This newer blood brought better looks to the horses in this country.

Connemaras It seems easiest to consider the breeds in alphabetical order which brings the one Irish breed, Connemaras, first. They are thirteen hands to fourteen hands two inches in height and their home is in the Connaught mountains, bogs, and rocky places where living conditions are very hard for man and beast. Therefore they are very tough, sure-footed and sensible, they are also docile and co-operative and make first-class hunters and jumpers. Grey is their most usual colour, also palamino, bay, brown-roan and black, but chestnut is not liked and piebalds and skewbalds are barred from the stud-book.

They should have seven to eight inches of bone, stand on short legs, have good riding-type shoulders with

A DARTMOOR CHAMPION *This typical Dartmoor with such a beautiful front is helping himself out of the handsome silver bowl he has just won*

heads and necks nicely set-on. Connemaras' heads have a degree of Arabian appearance coupled with a quiet calm expression; their eyes are gentle; quarters may be a little sloping in some of them. The grey, called "flea-bitten", is often to be found in these ponies, and it is not hard to see that many of the good Irish hunters, frequently also grey, have Connemara blood in them.

Dartmoors Dartmoor ponies do not exceed twelve hands two inches and are usually dark brown with plenty of mane and tail. They should have good long fronts, with an attractive outline, and short heads. As a rule their legs and feet are good and sturdy, but over-all they should be judged on riding principles: it is the good outline of the whole pony which can be called its distinguishing feature.

They can also be bay or grey, but for many years now Dartmoor ponies have been mixed with Shetland blood, so many bred on Dartmoor may be skewbalds. These, however, are not true ponies of the *breed* although now bred on Dartmoor.

Dales Dales ponies come from Northumberland and the neighbouring counties and are most liked when black and dark brown, although a grey or two can be seen. They are grand ponies, bred for power and activity, and have pony-type heads, very short, strong backs, good fronts and strong quarters. Their star performance is trotting and they are immensely strong and willing.

Their job used to be carrying very heavy loads of lead to Newcastle-on-Tyne from across the Dales. With plenty of mane, also fine hair on heels and up the back of their legs, once seen they are not hard to recognize again; it is probable that these sound, active ponies have not been tried out enough as crosses for hunters or jumpers.

Exmoors Possibly Exmoor ponies are the fastest (for their size), the gallop being very easy for them. They are easy to recognize with their well-known "mealy" or pale-shaded muzzle, the same shading appearing round the eyes, inside the thighs and on the forearms. The muzzles are very striking and in a true-type herd quite uniform. Their ears are lined with the pale colour too and are short and stubby. Their eyes are large (they are locally called "Toad-eyed") with a bright alert expression which indi-cates the life and vitality of this age-old breed which has grown a second coat of long hairs to drain the water off in winter!

Exmoor ponies are some of the best to grade up from, for hunter breeding; in the third generation a fine animal will result, but few people have the patience or unselfishness to look so far ahead and make use of our fine heritage of native, and therefore truly sound, animals. But it must be said that there are now more breeders using this splendid blood for the pur-

THE STURDY EXMOOR *Just as this breed has done for hundreds of years, the Exmoor carries an ordinary adult with no difficulty*

59

A GOOD FELL MARE *The kind expression is typical of this famous and useful breed which is always so generous and willing, whether hunting, in harness or carrying loads over rough country*

pose. Rich bay is Exmoor's usual colour.

Fells Near neighbours to the Dales are the Fell ponies but of quite a different touch for these are good ponies to ride and hunt although, of course, they too have the background of generations of heavy packwork, two hundred and forty miles a week with about sixteen stone.

Fell ponies have a wonderful walk; long-striding and rhythmic, sure-footed, of course, like all these ponies bred, for use and a long life, by our ancestors. With very long thick manes and tails flowing, hair on the heels—but not so much as the Dales—fine shoulders and comparatively long in the back, usually *very* black, the Fell pony is one of the easiest to recognize. The great manes and tails should be silky and the coats very bright giving a whole effect of shininess. In height they are about thirteen hands two inches to fourteen hands and are good safe rides for children or the elderly.

Highlands For sheer weight-carrying the Highland ponies exceed all others for they carry the deer on the moors and these weigh seventeen stone and more. The ponies are able to get over the ground at an incredibly fast pace under this great weight.

Grey is their most usual colour but there are a number of duns and reddish duns with often the dark "eel stripe" down the spine and at the back of the knees. Highland ponies' heads are short with good width between the eyes and in the jaw bone. They have small ears, and a quiet expression; often the Arab blood of long ago shows in their heads.

The mainland type is rather heavier than the Western Isles type. The latter are much liked for riding and make good hunters. This is borne out by the famous Three-day Event horse *High and Mighty* whose sire is a thoroughbred but his dam is half-Arab and half-Highland, with the Highland blood showing very clearly even to the "eel stripe" down his strong back. Manes and tails are full with the hair not expected to be silky as with the Fells, but there is very little hair on the heels. Highlands are very well ribbed-up with great broad quarters and strong thighs, big-boned with broad knees; everything to make for strength. Norwegian ponies are very like Highlands especially about the head and because of their colour, but the British pony is the more attractive and certainly more active.

HIGHLAND STALLION *A good example of the great strength of this breed. Notice his excellent front, short head and splendid bone*

New Forest The ponies of the New Forest are almost as famous to the ordinary person as are Shetlands, for the thousands who motor through the New Forest are very interested to see dozens of the ponies by the roadside showing no fear of cars and lorries. For some years now breeders have been keeping this breed pure, but it has to be admitted that they are of very mixed blood because years ago several people had their own ideas as to the best type to encourage and put out various stallions in the Forest according to their individual whims. There were Arabs and thoroughbreds, Welsh and Highlands and perhaps others. To this day the Highland influence can be seen in some ponies, the Arab in others especially in some blacks, and the Welsh in some greys as would be expected. But there is now a very good type becoming fixed and this is a nice riding pony full of common sense and reliability, about twelve hands two inches to fourteen hands; this is possibly as good a "family" pony as one can get.

Some time ago it used to be said of these ponies that they had ugly, big heads and sloping quarters but this is not true today. The New Forest pony is a deep-girthed, hardy, small hunter type able to go well in the average country. Bay or brown are the most usual colours but Forest ponies can be any colour and they are judged on riding pony lines. There is not so much "type" to consider in this breed.

Shetlands Everybody knows something about a Shetland pony, in fact some people even have a habit of calling *every* small equine a Shetland. Forty inches high at three years they must not exceed forty-two inches when grown up. Black is the favourite colour, but Shetlands can be any colour including skew- or pie-bald, having shining fine coats in summer and a very protective double winter coat which they are late in shedding. They have broad foreheads and deep jowls, neat ears, plenty of hair in the mane and tail; the latter looking somehow "important" as the ponies bustle away from you. They should indeed give an appearance of activity in their walk, moving with a quick flashing look. Shetlands are amazing

THE TINY SHETLAND *Only 42 inches high, once seen they are never forgotten. The head should be neat, as this one is, and they are never clumsy*

NEW FOREST *In the opinion of many, the ideal children's pony, being kind, easily broken and a good jumper and hunter*

trotters and some very good times have been recorded for them.

Many references have been made through the centuries in various records of Shetlands taken abroad, often for circus work and fairs. Frequently their small size and great strength was remarked upon quite correctly, for many thousands did hard work in the mines, they also carried the Shetland islanders and did the farmwork—all on a meagre ration and in a fierce climate. The demand for these ponies abroad is very great today, and very high prices are being paid especially for mares.

Welsh Last in the pony alphabet is the Welsh pony, one of the most lovely of all our breeds. The Welsh stud-book is divided into sections not always clear to some people. First in the book is Section A. Welsh mountain ponies which must not exceed twelve hands. Ponies in this section can be called the "cream" and all registrations are carefully examined and checked. Very

WELSH MOUNTAIN PONIES *A champion group which shows you the type better than a single picture could. They make, perhaps, the most attractive ponies of all, for the show ring*

Arab-like, these ponies should have a "dished" profile, large bright eyes, deep jawbones, lean faces coming down to fine-skinned muzzles with well-opened nostrils, small fine ears (small ears are especially prized), shapely necks, very good fronts, good well-sprung ribs and strong quarters, making a total of a robust pony coupled with great beauty. They should be on short legs with good bone and joints without any sign of "legginess".

Action has always been a great feature of the Welsh; in the olden days higher knee action was encouraged and the ponies were shod and trained to lift the knee but this is not natural to them and now a normal, very free action is expected with the appearance of great activity and movement in every joint and no sign of stiffness anywhere. A Welsh pony in action is a lovely sight if he is going with the definite precision and fine freedom which is his heritage.

These small ponies have won the highest honours at the biggest shows, often beating the much larger "blood" types for top awards. Grey is their most usual colour, but there are bays and palaminos, also brown and chestnut, but never pie- or skew-balds. There are some "wall" or blue eyes in some blood lines; this does not count against the ponies but at the same time there are some people who do not like it.

In Section B. there are Welsh ponies (you leave out the word "mountain" here) and these can be up to thirteen hands two inches, this section being opened in the first place for mountain ponies which grew more than twelve hands, breeders hoping to grade up a good sort of riding pony of the bigger size. There are not many of these ponies yet but they are good and it will be nice when there are more of them.

Section C. is for Welsh ponies of *cob* type, which means, of course, the rather stronger pony, again up to thirteen hands two inches. This sort of Welsh make splendid hunter ponies; they jump wonderfully well, are safe and sure on their feet, requiring little specialized care provided, of course, they are not asked to live in some small over-crowded little enclosure where they cannot fend for themselves.

The last section in this book is Section D. for Welsh cobs which get to a height of about fourteen hands two or three inches and are in appearance the basis of all weight-carrying cobs you ever see in the show-ring or in old pictures. With bright eyes, good heads and nice expressions, cobs are well "built-up" in front, a more powerful edition of the ponies from whom, in the first place, they were bred.

All Welsh have some hair on the heels but not very much and it is never curly. Cobs can trot very fast and are very popular at the shows for this. They jump magnificently as is shown by one of our best show jumpers, *Nugget*, a winner at the biggest shows.

Section E. in the book is just for geldings from *all* the other sections. This is a valuable list because it shows which families are producing the best ponies for the shows.

Each of the lovely native breeds have their special types impossible to describe on paper; examine them carefully when you see good ones; look at the expression of their faces and their kind of action as well as their general shape and you will soon know them at a glance and even be able to spot the likely crosses in ponies that have been bred from them.

When buying a registered pony care should be taken to see the transfer of the registration is made properly, otherwise the pony will be lost to its stud-book.

Finally, although it is often said they "live on nothing", the "nothing" does not mean small, dirty little bits of land. It means rougher places, heath or down, hill or gravel areas, what is left when the cows have gone over the land or the edges of plough-land. Give them space and variety but avoid rich modern pastures as much as you can.

CHAPTER SEVEN

Pit Ponies

BILL ACKROYD

FACTS AND FIGURES · TYPES OF PONIES · STABLING · FUN
AND GAMES · ILLNESS · MINERS' AFFECTION FOR THEIR
PONIES · AGE AND RETIREMENT · WORKING HOURS · LEGAL
SAFEGUARDS

*At the Horse of the Year Show each October there is always a parade of pit ponies
and it is one of the most popular items in the show. But there always seems to be a
good deal of misunderstanding about pit ponies; all sorts of silly stories are told
and all sorts of people will tell you that pit ponies are blind, get no fresh air, or
die after a year or two in the mines. All this, of course, is rubbish. Because so
many children really do want to know about pit ponies we asked Bill Ackroyd,
who has been with the National Coal Board for many years, is now its Publicity
Officer, and who really knows the* facts, *to tell us all about them.* Editors

THERE ARE ABOUT 10,000 pit
ponies and colliery horses working
in the mines today. Before 1842,
women, boys and girls were used to
pull or push the tubs of coal, but the
Act of Parliament known as the 1842
Mines Act forbade the use of women
and girls underground and restricted
the use of boys. As a result, ponies
were used in increasing numbers and,
before the First World War, over
70,000 horses and ponies were at work
in the mines.

As the mines become more and
more mechanized so the number of
ponies used falls; since 1947 the total
has dropped from 21,000 to 10,000.

About half of the 10,000 are in the
Northumberland and Durham coalfields. Here the seams of coal are thin
and it is customary to use ponies vary-
ing from ten to twelve hands. These
are Shetland and Welsh ponies.

In Yorkshire and the Midlands,
where the seams are thicker, ponies of
the Dales and Welsh cob breeds,
measuring up to fourteen hands are
used.

In the South Wales coalfields,
where the roadways are higher, they
are called colliery horses and measure
from thirteen to fifteen hands or over.
These are a cross between Welsh
cobs and shire horses.

There are no ponies in the mines in Kent or in Lancashire and very few in Scotland and North Wales. No mares are used underground.

Ponies can still be useful underground even with mechanized mining, as they can take materials along the airways on a simple rail-track, leaving the main roads free for the coal to be brought out by conveyors or locomotives. They will go anywhere where the road and their drivers lead them under proper conditions. In fact, one pony was adopted by a family after his working days were over and on the first day followed the daughter of the house indoors and upstairs into the bathroom!

In their underground stables, built in the intake airway, the ponies breathe the fresh air straight from the surface. The stables are electrically lit, with concrete or brick floors, and here they are cleaned and groomed daily and fed with regular, properly balanced food, which is specially treated to make sure it is free of dust.

Incidentally, the popular idea that pit ponies go blind is quite untrue. Blind ponies are not allowed to work in the mines under any circumstances.

The stables are in the charge of horsekeepers; by law, at least one to every fifteen ponies but, in practice, generally one to every eight.

A new pony first receives several weeks' training on the surface. When he enters a colliery, after being

Underground stables

examined and tested for glanders, at the age of four years or older (but not before) the pony receives skilled attention from his horsekeeper and is the subject of a daily report. At least once a year he is examined by a veterinary surgeon and at least twice a year by Horse Inspectors employed by the Ministry of Power.

The pony's driver takes him to work and feeds and waters him during the shift. You can see from the photographs the kind of protective harness

67

Harness and tub

he wears. The driver must report to his immediate superior and to the horsekeeper any accident that may happen or any matter that affects the pony's well-being. This must also be passed on to the manager or under-manager.

Miners become greatly attached to their ponies and are naturally in the habit of taking in titbits. The ponies are not beyond helping themselves to a snack out of the pocket of a coat hanging up. At one show, one of the ponies had a reputation for laughing after he had been given a sweet. A lady fed him biscuits and chocolates for several minutes without any response. In disgust she turned round to talk to her husband and the pony turned his head, lifted the flower from her button-hole, ate it, and then laughed.

Another pony loved to have a daily game with the stable brush after his shift. It had to be left across his path so that he could pick it up in his mouth and take it into the stall.

If a pony should go sick, he is treated underground, or taken to the surface, if it is going to be a long job.

"Nut" and "Nat". Note the shield for eye and head

If there is an accident underground the miners go to great lengths to save their ponies. Only a few years ago two Northumberland miners lost their lives in a gallant but unsuccessful attempt to save their pony from being overcome by mine gas after an accident.

On another occasion, when a pony was "barred in" by a fall of stone, his driver made daily trips under dangerous conditions to give him food and water till the fall was cleared.

Pit ponies have been shown regularly at the Royal Show and at Harringay during the past few years and their bearing and condition always cause favourable comment.

Compared with thousands of ponies that live out all the year round, on the mountains or the moors, the pit pony, in an even temperature underground all the year round, is well off. There he is not bothered by flies and insects, overpowering heat in summer or ice and snow in winter, and he does not have to fend for himself.

A pony continues to work as long as he is fit. The average working life is from ten to fifteen years, but there

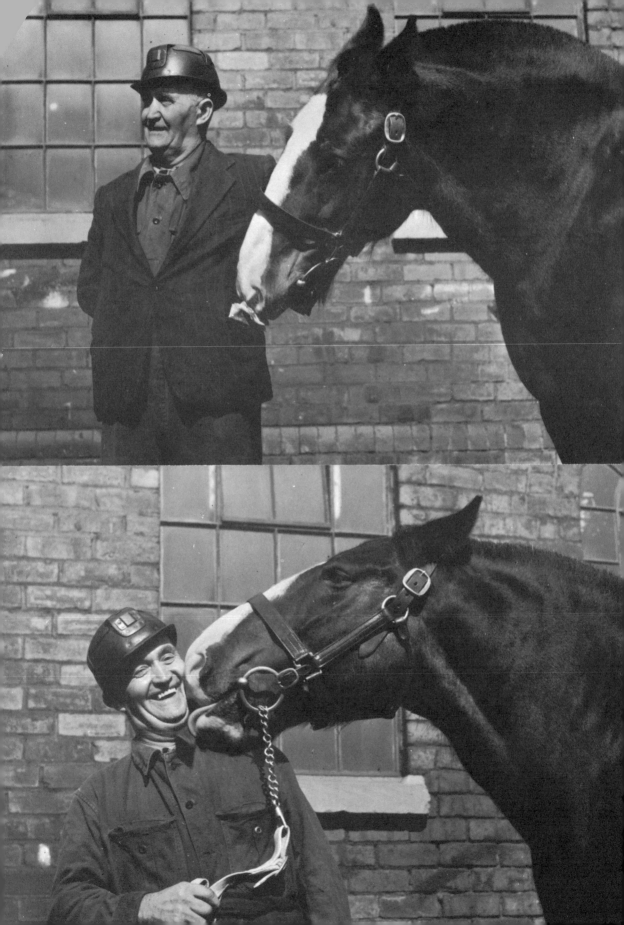

That's a good one! Steve from Lynmouth

elping himself. Taff, a Welsh colliery horse with ideas of his own. "Taffy was a Welshman!"

hank you

Holiday time in Wales

are some twenty-year-olds still doing light jobs. There is even said to be record of one that reached the age of thirty-four.

In some cases it is possible, with the help of the R S P C A, to have a retired pony adopted by an animal-lover. The National Coal Board do not sell old ponies for fear that they may fall into the hands of an unscrupulous dealer, so if no home can be found they are humanely destroyed under supervision.

The hours of work for a pit pony are laid down by law. A forty-eight hour week is the maximum allowed, except in cases of accident or saving life.

Some ponies are brought to the surface during the annual holiday in summer. But they are generally from the shallower pits. In the deeper mines where the temperatures are warmer there is a danger of the variable climate above ground affecting the ponies' health.

The pit pony is still doing a real job and, though the numbers are dropping steadily over the years as mechanization increases, it seems certain that they will continue to work for many years yet, giving to man their strength and companionship, as horses have done through the ages, in exchange for the care and attention which is now their right, since no other horse, working for its living, is protected by such detailed legislation.

B. J. Akroyd

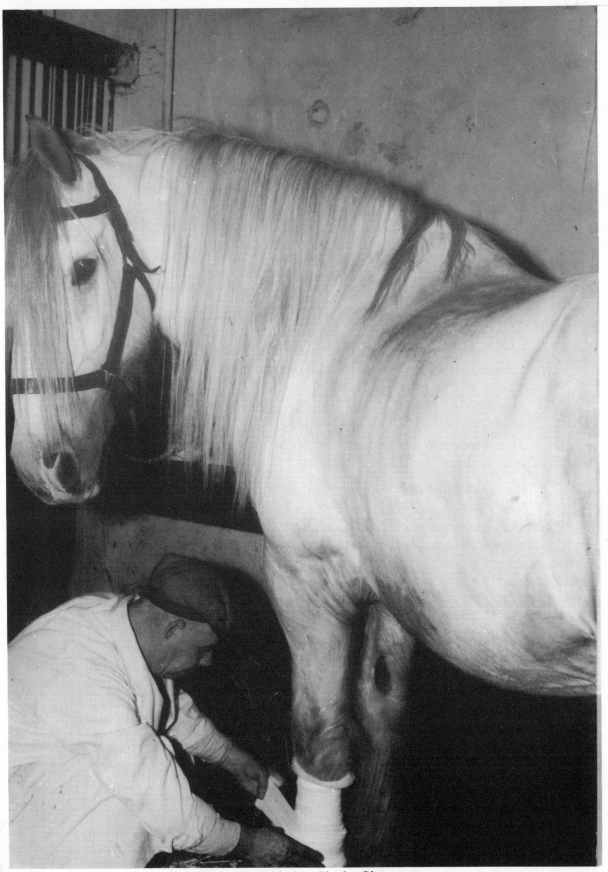

The horse hospital at Tondu, Glamorgan

CHAPTER EIGHT

The Riding School

DOUGLAS MOULD

LOCALITY · TYPE OF PONY · FEEDING · BREAKING ·
VOICE · PUPILS · ROUTINE

There are well over a thousand riding schools in Britain and it is probably true to say that more children get their riding at one of these schools than in any other way. We thought that it would be interesting, therefore, to talk about riding schools a little, not from the point of view of the children that go along once a week for a ride or a lesson, but from the point of view of the people who run them. Few people work harder for very little reward other than the satisfaction of seeing their pupils do well and there are few people to whom we should be more grateful, because they are helping to ensure that ponies and horses and riding are still loved in our country although we live in such a mechanical age.

We have asked Mr Douglas Mould who has been connected with horses all his life and who has run his school for many years to tell us about running a riding school. Editors

FROM MY EXPERIENCE I have learnt that there are five important aspects of running a riding school which always have to be borne in mind.

Locality

Unless it is a good indoor school in the middle of a town it is best to have premises where there are fields or suitable country adjoining. Here it is possible for your pupils to go out for rides and it is also possible for you to turn your ponies out to grass. It is quite feasible to keep the right type of pony out at grass all the year round, as long as you remember that in winter he needs extra fodder.

Type of Pony

Now as to the type of pony in a school; the first consideration, in my opinion, is constitution. That is to say, we must have something strong and hardy, I have always found that you cannot do better than our stalwart native breeds — Moorland, Welsh, New Forest, and others—they have been reared in their wild state and seem more likely, therefore, to stand up to outside conditions. They are also friendly and easy to handle.

OFF FOR A RIDE   *A typical Riding School scene at any week-end in any part of the country*

The sort of pony you will buy for a riding school depends a little on your circumstances. If you have good paddocks you can buy young, unbroken ponies, which, of course, are much cheaper, and leave them out at grass until they are ready to break in.

If, on the other hand, you wish to purchase ponies which are already trained, it is better to go to a respectable dealer, farmer or private stable where the children have outgrown their ponies. It is, of course, essential when buying to be sure that the ponies are really suitable. They should never be ridden by the pupils until they have been thoroughly tried. Obviously the most important thing in a riding school pony is temperament.

Feeding

This is very important too because temperament is largely controlled by it. It all depends, of course, on the amount of work that is expected of the pony. If in hard work, a little corn should be added with chaff, apart from hay or grass; but corn must always be used with discretion, for nobody wants a pony that is too gay— after all most ponies in a school will be carrying novices.

We must never forget that ponies do not only have to eat; they have to drink and, therefore, in organizing one's stable one must always see that the buckets are regularly filled or, if the ponies are out in paddocks, that the water supply is adequate. (In

75

SIMPLE INSTRUCTION *First things first: how to mount.* Below: THE PUPIL, *only a beginner, but already the benefits of simple instruction are evident*

winter the tank, or even the stream, can easily freeze up.)

Breaking in

If one has bought cheap ponies un-broken, the temptation is to back (put a rider on) them too early; this is certainly not advisable until they are three. The best plan for breaking is to begin by placing a bit in the pony's mouth, one with keys if possible, to give it something to play with. The bit is attached to a bridle or head collar and loose reins from the bit are fixed to a surcingle. At first, the bit

LONG REINS *Mr Mould, the author of this article, is a great believer in breaking in his riding school ponies by driving them on the long reins. This teaches them to go* forward

should only be in his mouth for an hour or so, and only when he is in a loose box. After a week he can be taken out on long reins; that is, a rein on each side of the pony long enough for you to walk behind him.

You can then persuade him to go forward with a flick of the reins on his side, and ask him to go back by a gentle pull on the bit.

Your *voice* should play quite an important part in breaking in a pony, and he will quickly become accustomed to it.

When you have had the pony on long reins for a week or two and you consider him controllable, then you can place a saddle on his back, still using the long reins for a time.

By now it should be possible to put a good child on the pony's back, or, better still, a lightweight adult. This

first rider must never, of course, be an inexperienced pupil. The value of breaking and backing your own ponies for your school is that then you know the ponies have been properly handled from the start and

BACKING *Once, the young pony has been backed it is led quietly round, still on the lunge to get it used to the saddle and the weight on its back*

THE BEAUTY-PARLOUR *Brushing out the mane—on both sides : even a rough, unclipped pony can be made to look smart and tidy*

MANICURE *Proper attention to the feet every day and whenever a pony goes out can save much trouble. Note the correct way of handling foot*

MUCKING OUT *An essential routine in any stables. The unsoiled straw is lifted well clear of the floor, shaken and replaced, loose and fresh*

are, therefore, likely to be more suitable.

The rider, having mounted, should sit for a short time, patting the pony on neck and sides before asking him to move off. That, of course, is the moment when the rider must be prepared for all eventualities. He must be sure, if it is humanly possible, to remain on top—sometimes easier said

one should always be holding a leading rein. The worst is now over and, with patience, all should now progress satisfactorily.

Pupils

Many of those attending riding schools, of course, just go for the ride. They do not really want proper instruction. The ones who really matter,

THE YARD *The best run schools, and indeed all the best stables, take great pride in having a spotless yard. This means hard work, especially with cobbles where not only can dirt of every sort collect, but weeds quickly grow. In the best run establishments there are "yard days" at least once a week*

than done! If a pony puts you off on the first occasion he is mounted, he will certainly try it again, but if the rider remains on top the pony will probably not attempt it further. During these proceedings, however, some-

if one is to be successful in a school, are the beginners.

I always think that the first thing is for the young rider to make his or her pony's acquaintance. Let them pet the pony, talk to him, lead him

THE STABLES *A typical Riding School scene, which always gives pleasure as one enters a yard.*
Loose boxes and a variety of heads: quality, ugly, sensible—but all kindly and generous

around on a halter: in other words gain confidence. The pony should be bridled and saddled *in the child's presence*, everything being fully explained: the use of the equipment and the name of everything. Then the child should be made to mount and dismount several times, being taught the proper deportment and the proper position. Then, how to hold the reins and the correct position of the legs—all this while the pony is standing still. The walk, the trot and the canter will follow automatically and after a dozen lessons the average child should really have made fair progress. It is so important not to want to learn too quickly.

These then are, as I see it, the five essentials in running a riding school. But of this I am sure, no riding school (or stable for that matter) can be run properly without good stable-management. However, this has been dealt with elsewhere so I will only remind you that it entails early morning watering and feeding, mucking out, grooming, midday and evening feeding, exercising, tidying up the yard, cleaning and caring for the equipment. And all that means *hard work*.

But no one who is afraid of hard work should have anything to do with a riding school.

Douglas Mould

CHAPTER NINE

The Gymkhana Pony

COLONEL JACK BULLEN

ORIGIN · PRINCE PHILIP CUP · GOOD ALL-ROUND PONY ·
TRAINING · REWARDS · HINTS FOR RIDERS · GOOD CONDI-
TION · SUITABLE EVENTS

Every Saturday, all over the country, from Easter until September, there are literally hundreds of gymkhanas being held, and literally thousands of children and ponies take part. In fact, it is probably true to say that for the majority of children who ride it is the gymkhana that provides them with most of their fun.

But, because the emphasis is on fun it would be a mistake to forget that, just like any other form of riding, it cannot all be left to chance. Proper schooling and preparation is necessary, and that goes for the rider as well as the pony! We have asked Colonel Bullen to give you a few hints about this.

He is famous in the Pony Club for the wonderful displays he has organized, and he has had, until recently, at his home in Dorset, some sixty ponies. His house is always swarming with children whom he is teaching to ride. He and Mrs Bullen, who as Ann Bullen is well known for her pictures of ponies and horses, have a large family of their own. Their eldest daughter Jenny is now an outstanding juvenile rider, who has won not only at the White City and Harringay, but also in Canada and America. Now Jane and Sarah are following in her footsteps. As you would expect, they do not only ride in shows, hunter trials and gymkhana competitions: they chiefly ride for fun.

Riding must never be taken too seriously. No one must ever mind if he or she doesn't win: if that is how they feel then it isn't fun any longer. Now read what Colonel Bullen has to tell you about preparing for gymkhanas, so that you can get even more fun out of them. Editors

YEARS AGO, when the British Army was in India, gymkhana events or mounted games were an energetic and amusing adjunct to garrison life. The soldiers' mounts in those days were usually polo ponies, which were beautifully trained and ideal for these events. In England, until recently, gymkhana events were almost always the Cinderella of small country shows,

Some of the Bullen family, both ponies and riders being beautifully turned out. Notice how they all wear caps as every child should, especially in Gymkhanas. A cap can save a nasty accident

only held if time permitted or if there were sufficient entries in the classes. Now, however, the Prince Philip Cup competition, introduced by His Royal Highness last year at the Horse of the Year Show, has put a very different complexion on things. Because of this competition the cheaper, more ordinary pony now also has a chance of becoming a star, in this new sphere.

When looking for a pony for gymkhana events, one should look for a good, all round pony; one which is an excellent hunter, a pleasant hack, and one that will give the rider any amount of fun. Some of the best places for buying inexpensive ponies are the native pony sales, New Forest ponies being particularly easy to break, as they are already so used to

people and are quiet with traffic. Moreover, they are a large breed, and will make fourteen hands two inches, as will the Connemaras. The best all round pony we ourselves have ever owned is a twelve hands two inches Exmoor, but he is rather an exception for his size. Care must be taken at sales not to be "had" by cheap, broken ponies, as often they turn out to be unmanageable and even rogues, which may be why they end up in the sale yard.

When buying a pony with a view to riding it in gymkhanas, do not choose one that is of a nervous or excitable temperament as these are, naturally, more difficult to break and school. Almost any pony will be inclined to "hot up" when it has been trained for mounted games. This is necessary up to a point, as the pony must be keen and quick off the mark, but one that is too highly strung may easily become wild and unmanageable. On the other hand, a stuffy, indolent pony is, more or less, useless, except for young children to learn on—for this, of course, it is invaluable.

If you are keen and wish to start training your young pony, do not neglect any part of his early training as this is the foundation of any work you will do with him in the future. To hurry this training will only result in spoiling the pony. He must learn to accept a snaffle bit, flexing his jaw correctly and going freely forward with nice, even strides. He must be able to turn in a correct and balanced manner. It would be entirely wrong to expect him to compete in gymkhana events before he can carry out these movements correctly. The result would be the sorry spectacle of a bewildered and unbalanced pony being hauled round by the head, whereas your aim should be that he will turn easily off his hocks, as does a well-schooled polo pony.

When training for mounted games, start at the walk, getting the pony used to every imaginable strange object, such as balloons, umbrellas, and washing lines. Give him rewards and encouragement to start with; remember the saying—"the horse and the elephant never forget". If you can possibly avoid it, never let your pony have a fright. It is sure to be your undoing later on, when he will have an attack of nerves at an awkward moment. With a young pony, entered in his first competitions, be sure to take him quietly and do not get him worried and upset. The aim is not to win, but to introduce your pony to the different events. There will be plenty of opportunities to work up to a faster performance once he has got the hang of things. A great deal of practice will, of course, be necessary before you can expect a really efficient pony. You must enter in as many competitions as you possibly can, but do put in plenty of quiet practice at home before going to shows: this is extremely important, and to do so will pay you in the long run. There are many tips to be learnt concerning gymkhana riding, such as not having your reins over the pony's head when you have to jump off and lead in a hurry and being able to vault on or mount equally well from either side. Remember, a quick and nippy (and quick-witted!) rider makes a quick and nippy pony.

All actual schooling should be done at home; this includes "schooling" the jockey as nothing can be more exasperating for a well-trained pony than to stand by and watch his inefficient rider making a mess of bobbing for the apple!!

Make sure that your pony is always

well turned out and in good condition; the gymkhana pony should not be the whiskery and badly-groomed creature he so often is. See that your saddlery is sound and supple as a result of correct care and attention. Pay great attention to your pony's feet, too; see that the shoes are firm and that there are no risen clenches.

At shows, make sure that your pony is supplied with a hay-net and water. Do not use him as a grandstand all day and then expect him to be at his best for the gymkhana events at the end. Do not wear spurs for these events and do not use a whip.

Finally, try always to be a cheerful and enthusiastic competitor and a

DRESS INFORMAL   *But still a hard hat*

good sporting loser—you will then be an asset to any team, I am sure. The Prince Philip Cup was introduced to give every child who is not the owner of either a show pony or a show jumper the chance of competing at a big London show, and I, for one, hope that this event will never become too professional and so cease to be staged for the fun of it.

Gymkhana Games particularly suitable for team events such as the Prince Philip Cup

Team Relay Bending Race   A relay race in which the riders have to weave round a line of bending posts.

The Potato Picking Scramble   The riders have to collect potatoes, one at a time, from the centre of the arena, and drop them into their team's buckets. Two members of each team ride for a stated time, followed by the other two members of each team. The team which collects the greatest number of potatoes in the time allowed is the winner.

The Laundry Race   Two members of each team have to gallop from the start to the line to hang up their washing and then return with the empty basket to their second pair. These then have to collect their washing and the first team past the finish with a complete set of washing and pegs is the winner.

Musical Sacks (or Hats)   Played like Musical Chairs, the riders have to gallop to the centre and stand on a sack (or put on a hat) when the music

stops. A rider eliminated in the first round scores one point for his team, a rider eliminated in the second round scores two points, and so on. The team whose riders gain the greatest total score is the winner.

The Balloon Race   No. 1 of each team has to collect a balloon from the far end of the arena and return to hand it to No. 2. No. 2 has then to take this balloon and collect another, handing both on to No. 3, and so on. The winning team is the one whose No. 4 first crosses the finish with four balloons.

The Egg and Racquet Race   No. 1 of each team has to carry an egg on a tennis racquet round a set of three bending posts and return to hand them to No. 2. Nos. 2, 3 and 4 do the same, handing the egg on the racquet to each other in succession. The winning team is the one whose No. 4 is first past the finish with an egg on the racquet. Should an egg be dropped, the rider must collect another egg from the container on the middle pole, starting again from the place where the egg was dropped.

The Economy Stakes   No. 1 has to lead his pony to his saddle, put it on, girth up using two buckles and ride round four bending posts to No. 2. He gives the saddle to No. 2 and can help him to saddle up. No. 2 then rides round the bending poles to No. 3. Similarly No. 3 saddles up, rides to No. 4, who has to complete the course with the same saddle on his pony. The winning

team is the one whose No. 4 is first past the finish, mounted.

The Grooms' Race No. 1 has to lead No. 2's pony round four bending posts and then hand it to No. 2. No. 2 must mount his own pony and similarly lead No. 3's pony to him. No. 3 must mount his own pony and lead No. 4's pony to him. No. 4 must mount his own pony and lead No. 1's to the finish. The winning team will be the one whose No. 4 is first past the finish.

The Sack Race No. 1 has to ride to the centre line, dismount, get into a sack, lead his pony to No. 2 at the other end of the arena and hand the sack to him. No. 2 has to gallop to

86

all the excitement and atmosphere of the great event which is the blue riband of gymkhanas

the centre line carrying the sack, dismount, get into the sack and lead his pony to No. 3. Similarly No. 3 and then No. 4 have to complete the course. The winning team is the one whose No. 4 is first past the finish in the sack and leading his pony.

Uncle Tom Cobley Stakes No. 1, carrying a pint pot, rides bareback round bending posts to the end of the arena, where he picks up No. 2 on to his pony and they both ride back to the start. Here they hand the pint pot to No. 3 who similarly rides to pick up No. 4. The winning team is the one whose No. 3 and 4 are first past the finish, mounted and carrying the pint pot.

John F. S. Bullen.

CHAPTER TEN

The Pony Club

CHRISTINE BLACK

ORIGIN · MEMBERSHIP · LOCAL BRANCHES · RALLIES ·
CAMPS · BRITISH HORSE SOCIETY; ITS OBJECTS

There is no doubt that the Pony Club has done more than any other organization to encourage children not only to ride, but also to look after their own ponies. This has meant that good horsemanship has been carried on with successive generations. Because of the Pony Club all sorts of children have been able to receive first-class instruction, which they might never have had otherwise.

There are, at present, over 40,000 members and many ex-members all over the world. Some of the most famous ex-members are Pat Smythe, Dawn Wofford, Sheila Wilcox, and Alan Oliver.

The Grafton Hunt branch was one of the original branches formed in 1928 and one of the editors of this book was one of the very first members of the Pony Club, as he, his brother and sister were among the founder members of the Grafton branch. There is no doubt that all ex-members of the Pony Club, whether famous or not, realize how much they owe to their Pony Club days. We thought that we could not do better than to invite Christine Black, who is the secretary of the Pony Club, to tell us something about it. Editors

THE IDEA OF the Pony Club was born some thirty-one years ago. In those days the horse had already been replaced by the motor as a means of transport and, apart from hunting, riding for recreation and pleasure had hardly come into its own. It really looked as though horses were in danger of dying out in this country.

The best way of keeping interest alive is to inspire the rising generation; this is just what the Pony Club did then, and is continuing to do now. The membership grew by leaps and bounds. Riding became more and more popular. Ponies and horses were bred in greater and greater number. Far from disappearing, there has never been a time when horses have enjoyed such popularity, among people from every walk of life. The

LOTS OF GIRLS

ONE BOY *But it seems that more boys, especially in the north of England, are now becoming keen on riding*

THE RIDES ASSEMBLE AT A RALLY *Three or four different rides for the different standards*

Pony Club has undoubtedly played a great part in this resurgence of interest. Today there are over 40,000 members in no less than seventeen different countries. Indeed the club can claim to rank among the leading youth organizations of our time.

What exactly is the Pony Club? It is a club open to all boys and girls under twenty-one years of age who are interested in ponies and riding. For a small entrance fee and an annual subscription, members join their local branch of the Club and take part in the activities arranged for them.

The branches correspond as far as possible with the hunting areas and are usually known by the same name as the Hunt in whose area they operate. There has always been this close link between the Pony Club and hunting. In addition there are a great many branches in areas near large towns where there is no hunting.

Each branch is run by a District Commissioner and a Local Committee. These, and the many other helpers and instructors, all give their time and the benefits of their experience to the Pony Club voluntarily. During school holidays the branches hold rallies which all members are expected to attend as often as they can.

PONY CLUB CAMP *Makeshift, but very adequate, lines set up in a park where a week's camp is being held*

91

INSTRUCTION *A ride lines up in groups awaiting instructions*

The rallies are varied and include mounted instruction, lectures, film shows, occasional gymkhanas, special meets of hounds, visits to places of interest and test days. The annual camp is the highlight of the year in most branches, for it is camping that provides the best opportunities for the aims of the Pony Club to be put into effect. In camp each member has complete charge of a pony (either his own, or one hired or borrowed for the occasion) and is taught to look after it correctly, to feed and groom it and to care for its saddlery. The riding periods alternate between instruction in a manège—the members being divided into "rides" according to their age and ability, jumping, games, and riding across natural country—e.g. mock hunts, paper chases, etc.

At all Pony Club rallies, the emphasis is on learning, through enjoyment. Riding is fun. Sharing its pleasures with others is fun, making new friends is fun—and fun not only for the members, but for the adults and, if the Pony Club's aims are properly applied, fun for the ponies too.

By no means all members are lucky enough to have ponies of their own and many hire a pony from their local riding school for the mounted rallies. Most riding schools are only too willing to co-operate with the Pony Club in this way.

The Pony Club is an integral part

93

Above: *Preparing for inspection before setting off for the ride*

Below: COMMUNAL GROOMING *Here the accommodation is in a barn, stalls being made by the use of hurdles*

The instructor explains about jumping

of the British Horse Society, which is the organization which looks after all the interests of horses and riders in this country. The headquarters of the Club are at 16 Bedford Square, London, W.C.1. From this address the general policy is conducted by the Pony Club Organization Com-

mittee. As well as administering the affairs of the Club and maintaining direct contact with the branches throughout the world, headquarters produces books and instructional publications, films, film strip lectures, Christmas cards, a diary, Club badges and ties. Courses are run for instruc-

The result of instruction. The ride looks on as each jumps in turn, first a simple brush fence . . .

tors, tests are organized, "Visiting Commissioners", who go round to Branches in turn, are appointed. A national Inter-Branch Competition and a Mounted Games Championship are organized. The Club's official handbook, which all instructors and examiners use and which all members would do well to read, is *Horsemanship for the Pony Club*.

What is there about the Pony Club that so many people should give their time and effort so willingly and unstintingly to help? Maybe it has something to do with the third section of its OBJECTS, which are:

95

. . . *then a little stile*

OBEDIENCE *Three jump together over hurdles with no wings. This is achieved by patient schooling and taking the pony steadily* (see Chapter IV)

TO ENCOURAGE YOUNG PEOPLE TO RIDE AND TO LEARN TO ENJOY ALL KINDS OF SPORT CONNECTED WITH HORSES AND RIDING.

TO PROVIDE INSTRUCTION IN RIDING AND HORSEMANSHIP AND TO INSTIL IN MEMBERS THE PROPER CARE OF THEIR ANIMALS.

TO PROMOTE THE HIGHEST IDEALS OF SPORTSMANSHIP, CITIZENSHIP AND LOYALTY, THEREBY CULTIVATING STRENGTH OF CHARACTER AND SELF-DISCIPLINE.

By taking part in such healthy, outdoor recreation; by learning to ride and understand horses and ponies, to care for them, to mix with others with similar interests; by the high standards set, Pony Club members are learning, in their free time and of their own free will, qualities that will stand them in good stead in their future lives.

G

Christine Pack

CHAPTER ELEVEN

Great Equestrian Events

B. L. KEARLEY

THE OLYMPIC GAMES · BADMINTON · BURGHLEY · PONY CLUB
CHAMPIONSHIPS · THE WHITE CITY · THE HORSE OF THE
YEAR SHOW · THE CLASSIC RACES · THE GRAND NATIONAL ·
THE WESTCHESTER CUP

*If your friends at school know that you are fond of ponies and riding you look
rather silly if they ask you some question like "What is the Three Day Event at
Badminton?" and you cannot answer them. A true lover of horses knows at least
something about all the big events in which horses play the chief part. Obviously
it is impossible to know everything about all these events, but it is, we think, a
help to know what they are. Here are some interesting facts about such events as
the Olympic Games, White City, Badminton.* Editors

THE MOST IMPORTANT horse events in the world today are undoubtedly the international equestrian competitions held in a different country every four years at the Olympic Games.

Olympic Games

The first of these is the Grand Prix (individual and team) dressage contest which requires many years of concentrated practice and the exercise of the greatest patience in both horse and rider before they can hope to compete.

Dressage Major St. Cyr of Sweden, riding *Juli*, was the winner at the last Games in Stockholm in 1956. He was also the winner at Helsinki in 1952, riding *Master Rufus*. In both years he was followed in second place by Madame Hartel riding *Jubilee* (on whom she gave a charming and delightful solo display to music at Harringay in 1955).

Three-Day Event The second Olympic competition is the International Three-Day Event (team as well as individual) which is an exhaustive trial of stamina and judgement for horse and man (women are not allowed to compete). On the first day there is a dressage test; on the second day an endurance, speed and cross-country test divided into separate

98

stages: roads and tracks, a steeple-chase course, a cross-country course and a finish on the flat, each phase having to be completed within a certain time limit. The last test—on the third day—is over a show jumping course. Horses are vetted throughout and to come through successfully they must be tough, bold and resolute, and combine maximum obedience with fluency of movement. Most important of all, they must start sound and finish sound.

Great Britain won this event in Stockholm from eighteen other countries in 1956, but we had some anxious moments when Her Majesty's *Countryman* came to grief at fence number 22, a post and rails set in a water-logged trench with steep and very slippery sides. *Countryman* slipped as he made his spring and landed with his fore-legs one side of the obstacle and hind legs the other side, with one hind leg trapped through the rails. Some Swedish soldiers stationed there immediately tried to pull him over forwards, which would have probably broken his leg but, on instructions from a spectator, his rider—Bertie Hill—managed to push him over backwards. Although this completely submerged the horse in the water it freed him and he was able to get up and Hill remounted. Then, at the second attempt, this courageous horse flew from bank to bank as if nothing had happened!

Our winning team at Stockholm consisted of Colonel Frank Weldon on his famous *Kilbarry*, Major L. Rook on *Wild Venture* and Mr. Bertie Hill on *Countryman*. It will be remembered that *Kilbarry* met with a tragic end brushing through the top of a flimsy-looking three foot six-inch brush fence (which was trappily backed by a stout but hidden pole) at the Cottesmore two-day event meeting the following year. A lesson—if ever there was one—that strong fences are the safest.

Place jumping The third Olympic contest is the Grand Prix des Nations, considered the *chef-d'oeuvre* of international show jumping, the winning team holding the title of World Champions for the next four years. The placings in 1956 were Germany first, Italy second and Great Britain (Mr. Wilf White on *Nizefela*, Miss Pat Smythe on *Flanagan* and Mr. Peter Robeson on *Scorchin*) third.

The greatest honour of that year's contest went to the Gold Medal winner—Herr Winkler—who jumped a final clear round on his beautiful mare *Halla* whilst suffering agony from a wrenched riding muscle.

The first Olympic Equestrian events after the Second World War were held in England in 1948. Great Britain was third in the Grand Prix des Nations (which was won on appalling wet going by Brazil) but eliminated in the Three-Day Event.

99

BADMINTON *Sheila Wilcox and* High and Mighty *have a clear round in the jumping on the third day and win for the second year running*

Badminton

It was then appreciated at once by the British Horse Society that if we were to have a chance of success in the future we must start training straight away. Steps were therefore taken to draw up a programme for the Three-Day Combined Training Competition. The Duke of Beaufort kindly offered facilities for such an annual contest on his Badminton estate, so now we come to the next greatest equestrian event — the Badminton Three-Day Horse Trials. This follows the pattern of the Olympic three-day, although at its inception the courses were not so severe.

Now, however, Badminton has achieved international status and the object of the British Horse Society (to found and foster combined training, previously confined to military riders, as a popular sport for civilians, thus enabling us to find and train horses and riders suitable to compete in the Olympics) has been more than justified. Our win in 1956 at Stockholm alone is proof enough.

Although lady riders are barred from the Olympic three-day event it is remarkable how successful they are in our own competitions, and we must mention the remarkable feat of Miss Sheila Wilcox who won at Badminton on her horse *High and Mighty* in 1957 and 1958, scoring bonus marks beyond belief.

Burghley

Badminton was followed by a similar annual three-day event at Harewood, the home of the Princess Royal, and now two-day and one-day events are popular all over the country.

After the Three-Day Event at Harewood had been discontinued, a new event was staged at Burghley — thanks to Lord Exeter — and has become an outstanding success. It was also the venue of the 1966 World Championships.

HAREWOOD *For the first time a foreign competitor wins the Harewood Three-Day Event. Herr Pohlmann on* Polarfuchs

THE PONY CLUB CHAMPIONSHIPS *Dressage. Hundreds of competitors, but it is a lonely moment when you are doing your test on your own in the arena*

Captain Piero d'Inzeo, from Italy, on The Rock, *clearing the gaily beflowered water jump*

Pony Club Championships

Before leaving combined training we should notice the annual Pony Club Championships held at High Grove, Tetbury. 1958 was the tenth year that these championships have been held, during which period such an improved standard of riding has been developed that the tests have had to be made stiffer and stiffer. The Team Championship was won for the second year in succession by the Staff College and Sandhurst Branch against the finalists from twelve area competitions. East Kent was second, and North Norfolk third. The Pony Club competitions are the nursery from which our future champions will spring.

It is strange to reflect that although mechanization has ousted the horse from the sphere of utility, yet the general standard of riding—particularly in horse shows—is higher than it has ever been. Television has popularized show jumping with the public. As a result there are good gates and so good prizes.

103

Pat Smythe winning the Queen Elizabeth Cup on Mr. Pollard

The White City

Of the numerous shows the Royal International at the White City must take precedence. This show first began in London, at Olympia, in 1907, and continued there with an elegant, intimate atmosphere, under the eagle eye and personal direction of the late Lord Lonsdale (except during the First World War) until 1939, when war started again.

In 1946 it was appreciated by the organizers that if the International was to be revived and made a paying proposition a place must be found with sufficient seating capacity for the vast audience required. The White City was chosen, with very happy results.

The most coveted prize at the International is certainly the King George V Cup which has been won by many famous horses since its inception in 1911. Greatest of them all, however, must be Lieutenant-Colonel Harry Llewellyn's *Foxhunter* who won it in 1948, 1950 and 1953. The evening of the last year when *Foxhunter* won is

Junior Champion at the White City: Graham Mott on Mister Robin. Notice the firm contact of his knee on the saddle, and how his hands have eased up the neck to make sure that he does not jab his pony in the mouth. Compare this with d'Inzeo

remembered as "The Night of the Flood", for a cloud burst over Shepherds Bush, and it was touch and go whether the show could continue. Lieutenant-Colonel Jack Talbot-Ponsonby also holds the proud distinction of having won the King's Cup three times, but not on the same horse—twice with *Chelsea* (in 1930 and 1932) and finally, on *Best Girl* (in 1934) all, of course, at Olympia where, being under cover, rainstorms could not add to the hazards. This officer was a member of our three-day team at the Olympic Games in Berlin in 1936 when his horse fell at the pond fence and we lost—I think—some 1300 marks until this resolute rider caught his mount again. Even so we finished second to Germany.

A remarkable feature of the 1958 Royal International was the greatly improved riding by the American team which won the coveted Prince of Wales Cup which has been held by Great Britain since 1949, with the exception of 1955 when it was won by Italy. The American captain, Mr. W.

Steinkraus, won the King's Cup on *First Boy* in 1956; Mr. Hugh Wiley won it in 1958, on *Master William*. Will there be a third American victory this year?

The opposite number of the King's Cup (which is for men only) is the Queen Elizabeth II Cup for ladies. It is pleasing to record that at last in 1958, Miss Pat Smythe, riding *Mr. Pollard*, was the winner. Miss Smythe had won nearly every other competition open to her, but in this particular cup she had always, so far, been pipped on the post. The Queen Elizabeth Cup has been won twice by Miss Iris Kellet and by Miss Dawn Palethorpe, both of whom will probably be out for a third attempt this year.

The Sash of Honour was won on the first day and retained throughout the week by that beautiful Italian horseman, Captain Piero d'Inzeo, who carried off no less than five jumping prizes, and was second in the King's Cup.

The Saddle of Honour, for points gained on only one horse, deservedly went to Alan Oliver and *Red Admiral*.

Other events at the Royal International (Her Majesty graciously bestowed the title of "Royal" in 1957, the Show's Jubilee year) are the *Daily Mail* Champion Cup, the Champion Hunter Challenge Cup, the Champion Hack Challenge Cup, the Junior Jumping Championship, the Winston

Churchill Cup for the Supreme Champion Riding Horse (chosen by popular acclaim) and various Harness Classes.

Horse of the Year Show

The Horse of the Year Show at Harringay must also be counted as a great equestrian event, for in the ten years since it began it became such a general favourite, that it was impossible to obtain seats unless booked weeks ahead. As all horses competing, whether hunters, hacks or jumpers, have to be qualified by eliminating competitions throughout the show season, Harringay did really fulfil its function as first envisaged by its creator, the late Captain Tony Collings, of being a show of champions and a grand finale to the show season. Ted Williams won the British Show Jumping Association Spurs in 1958 for the fourth successive year, and Alan Oliver was awarded the Harringay Spurs, the equivalent trophy for points scored in international competitions. The Horse of the Year Show has now moved to Wembley stadium, where we hope it will continue to be the darling of the gods as well as the giants, human and equine.

Racing

As far as racing is concerned the major events of the calendar are the "Classics", on the flat, and the Grand

106

THE HORSE OF THE YEAR SHOW *Ted Williams, Leading Jumper of the year five times the Horse of the Year Show. Here he is riding* Pegasus, *whose splendid dapple colouring show up thrillingly in the spot-lights*

THE DERBY *The 1958 winner*, Hard Ridden, *C. Smirke up. Notice how spare he is compared with a show pony: how hard his muscles; almost like a greyhound*

THE GRAND NATIONAL *The 1958 winner*, Mr. What, *A. Freeman up. Compare him with the Derby winner and see if you can appreciate the differences between a great flat race winner and a great steeplechaser*

But it is not only in the Grand National that people have falls. Here is one at a point-to-point. Many of the best steeplechasers—horses and riders—get their first training in point-to-points. And part of their training is often a fall!

National and Cheltenham Gold Cup, over fences. The chief of the classic races, all of which are for three-year-olds only, is the Derby, run at Epsom during the first week in June. It was founded in 1780. Each horse has to carry nine stone, whereas the fillies in the Oaks carry 8 stone 9 lbs. Each race is run over one and a half miles.

The Grand National is run over four and a half miles and is a handicap, the top weight being as much as 12 stone 7 lbs. and the bottom weight as little as 8 stone 10 lbs. It is for horses of any age over five years and is run over the greatest course in the world at Aintree, near Liverpool.

It is interesting that the Grand National is run at an average speed of 28 m.p.h. and the Derby at

POLO *A mêlée round the goal. Often the posts are made of wicker*

32 m.p.h. (The average speed round a show jumping course is 20 m.p.h.)

The Cheltenham Gold Cup is over four miles, all horses carrying the same weight.

Other great flat races are the Ascot Gold Cup, the King George VI and Queen Elizabeth Stakes, the Prix de l'Arc de Triomphe, in France, and the Washington Stakes at Laurel Park, in America. These are all tests of **stamina open to horses of any age.**

Polo

Polo becomes increasingly popular each year, but so far the famous Westchester Cup, the match between Britain and America, has not been revived since the war.

B. L. Kearley

An action picture showing how handy, supple and courageous polo ponies have to be. It takes months of patient, careful schooling to train a pony. Notice the ponies' protective boots and their tails bandaged up so that they cannot obstruct other players. The riders wear helmets and their sticks are made of bamboo

CHAPTER TWELVE

Show Jumping on Television

DORIAN WILLIAMS

WHAT TO LOOK FOR · DIFFERENT STYLES · THE EXPERTS ·
BEHIND THE SCENES · THE PRODUCER · THE CAMERAS · THE
COMMENTATOR

Probably something like ten million people now watch show jumping on tele-vision. In fact, there is no doubt that its great popularity has done almost more than anything else to revive the interest, all over the country, in horses and ponies and riding. Thanks to television it is now possible for us to see the greatest horse-men and horsewomen, and the greatest horses in the world, to see them so regularly, what is more, that they almost become like old friends and we can recognize our favourites the moment we see them.

This, of course, means that we are also getting a wonderful opportunity to learn all sorts of things just from watching them. We thought that we would, therefore, include a chapter about watching show jumping on television, believing, too, that you might like to know a little of what goes on behind the scenes when a big show is being televised.　　　　　　　　　　　　　　Editors

I ALWAYS THINK that one of the reasons that show jumping is so popular on television is that with jumping it is possible to get absolutely *everything that matters* on the little screen of a television set. This is hardly pos-sible with any other sport, except perhaps tennis and boxing, which are equally popular. With football it is not always possible to tell whereabouts in the field the play is; with cricket it is not equally possible to see the fielders in the deep as well as the bats-men; with athletics and with racing,

unless the field is bunched very close together it is not possible to see any but the leader or leaders, nor how close they are to the finish; with golf it is not always possible even to see the ball. But with show jumping it is possible to see everything that mat-ters: the fence, the horse and the rider. It is even possible to glance quickly at the clock, if it is a jump-off on time. So all the interest and excite-ment is concentrated.

It is possible, too, for the producer and his cameras to give you more than

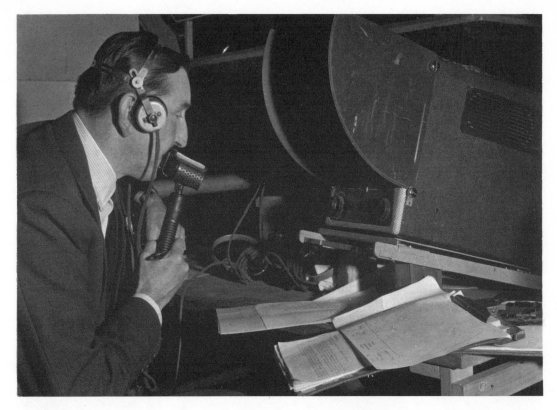

Dorian Williams giving a television commentary. He looks at the monitor set all the time

just the thrill of watching. Not only are you able to watch very carefully the way this competitor rides, or that horse jumps, you are also able to compare one with another.

For instance, supposing there are three fences down one side of the arena, a single fence—let's say a wall —and then about fifty feet or sixteen yards away a double fence, the first part being a white gate, the second part parallel poles. While we are watching the first horse or two go round we are told that the distance between the two parts of the double is twenty-six feet and that this is a distance which *should* be covered by one non-jumping stride. As we watch we see that most horses take two strides. Now why is this? The second part of the double, the parallel poles has a spread of five feet six inches, which is quite wide, and riders seem to be afraid that if their horse lands rather close to the first part he is going to find it very difficult to reach the second part in just one stride, or at any rate reach it sufficiently easily

H

FAMOUS JUMPERS, BRITISH *Compare all the different styles—Pat Smythe on Flanagan*

to be able to clear that five feet six inches spread. But by taking two strides he is getting too close to the parallel poles, and the horse knocks the first pole down.

Horse after horse, we notice, has a fault at the double. Then along comes one of the real top-notchers, Pat Smythe or Hans Winkler, or one of the d'Inzeo brothers, and they sail over it with the greatest of ease, and with only one stride in between. How did they manage it? If we watch very carefully on television we can see. The wall before the double is fifty feet away, about six strides for a normal striding horse. But suddenly we notice that the experts cover that distance in five strides. They approach the wall faster, so that they land well out over it. As soon as they land they increase their speed and lengthen their stride

114

Anne Townsend on Irish Lace

so that they can take off well up to the first part of the double—the gate. This means that they again land well out and can easily and naturally reach the parallel poles after one big stride. No difficulty at all.

But then comes Ted Williams, perhaps, or Alan Oliver; they may prefer a different method. Instead of six strides after the wall, they hook back —that is to say, check their mount— and take seven or even eight strides. By doing this they can time it so that they take off at exactly the right spot and then they know they will land fairly close after the gate which will give them room for two short, but strong, strides with gathering momentum, before the parallel bars. When *Nugget* arrives with his unbelievably short stride and strong massive quarters, he, believe it or not, manages to

115

bucket in *four* strides between the two parts of the double.

We can watch all these different styles and methods on television, if we know what to look for, and learn a lot from them.

For all this (the three fences down the far side) television is using a long-range lens in the camera. But let's change the lens and go in close. Now we can learn even more, because by watching carefully we can notice the different ways in which the different competitors ride. We notice how still Pat Smythe keeps her legs and how hard we shall have to look if we are to see just how she gives *Flanagan* or *Mr. Pollard* the aids. We notice how Ted Williams (swinging his body slightly and pressing one side of his mount's neck with the rein) makes the horse divert a little from the straight approach to the fence, so that he has just a few inches more, which

John Walmsley on Nugget

will prevent him from getting too close. We notice how d'Inzeo keeps his hands absolutely still at the base of his horse's neck so that the horse's head is always steady, which means that the animal is always balanced. We notice, too, how he just moves the wrist the fraction of an inch, giving his horse a little more rein and thus lengthening its stride. We notice how Peter Robeson has only the tip of his toe in the stirrups. We notice how Wilf White always has one hand slightly above the other, to help him steady the great *Nizefela*.

So much to learn if we watch carefully; more even than if we were privileged to stand at the side of the school and watch Pat Smythe training her horses at Miserden, or the d'Inzeos schooling in Rome. Much more, certainly, than if we are away up on the stand, too far off to see the detail that we can see on television.

H. G. Winkler on Orient

Alan Oliver on Red Star

Ted Williams on Pegasus

To bring this television to millions of viewers there is a great deal of work going on behind the scenes. In the first place, the producer and commentator get together with the show authorities to decide which is the best competition to televise.

Next, and this is important, it has to be decided how many cameras can be used, where they will be placed and what the principal function of each one will be. For instance, one camera will, if possible, be near the collecting ring, so that if there is a delay in the ring a picture can be shown of the riders waiting their turn. If a big fence, the wall, perhaps, obscures another fence that is behind it;

Piero d'Inzeo on Uruguay *again, but notice how he is still not interfering with his horse in any way though he has made a bad mistake at the 7 ft. wall*

then there must be another camera to cover that. The producer may want to have some interviews, so there must be a camera lined up outside for that. There must always be a reserve camera so that if any one should break down it is always possible to get at least a general picture.

Each camera's picture shows on one of the battery of monitor sets in the producer's scanner. By pressing the relevant button the producer puts up on to the master-monitor the picture he wants. This is the one that goes out to the viewers.

Producer and commentator get together some time before transmission to decide roughly how the cameras

Carlos Figueroa (Spain) on Gracieux

Raimondo d'Inzeo (Italy) on The Quiet Man. *It is impossible to fault horse or rider in this really lovely picture*

will be used: a general picture for the first two rounds so that the commentator can explain the course and the competition; the first three fences on "camera one" which is high up in the middle of the stand one side; the wall on "camera two", a head-on shot, and so on.

The commentator wears earphones, of course, and the producer is talking to him (as well as to the cameramen) all the time, though the commentator can never talk back because anything *he* says goes out all over the country. The commentator, too, you must remember, is commentating on what he sees in his monitor set. It is very important that he should remember this, otherwise he might be talking about something that the viewers

Bob Grayston (South Africa) on Buccaneer. He has just jumped over 7 ft. to win the South African High Jump record. (He also won the Hunter Championship on this horse: a real example of versatility)

Gonda Butters (*South Africa*) *on* Oerskiet

Hugh Wiley (U.S.A.) winning the Dublin High Jump on Nautical. Notice the sloping poles which ensures that the base of the fence, or ground line, is brought well out in front of the jump, thus ensuring a good take-off

THE TAKE-OFF, THE JUMP, THE LANDING *A composite picture showing Douglas Bunn in three phases of a jump*

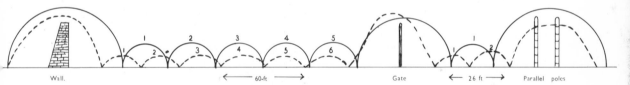

Wall.   ←— 60-ft —→   Gate   ← 26 ft →   Parallel poles

APPROACHING A DOUBLE *This diagram shows how one rider (dotted line) takes wall too slow, needs six strides to reach gate, does not clear gate sufficiently to reach poles in one stride, but by taking two strides gets too close to poles: while other rider (single line) takes five strides between fences, approaches gate faster and so can reach poles easily in one*

cannot see. And how that annoys them!

So the programme is built up and if all goes according to plan ten million viewers will see an hour, perhaps, of really good, exciting, spectacular jumping, with a thrilling jump-off as a finale. A few of those millions are, I hope, watching for what they can *learn* from seeing these great experts as close as if they were in the room. One will always learn more by watching the experts than by any other means. So may your viewing not only be interesting, but also instructive.

Dorian Williams

Conclusion

So THERE WE ARE. Time to close the stable door, have a last look round, and turn out the lights. Are you sure, before you go and get your own meal, that you have really attended to the needs of your pony? That, we believe, is the most important thing if one is lucky enough ever to have a pony of one's own. He is an animal, he can give enormous pleasure—but he is not a human being. He relies on you, his owner, to look after him. So make this your first duty. See that he has enough food and water. Remember that he has to be properly shod. Watch out for all the little ailments that he might be troubled by, especially if he is living out. *He cannot tell you about them.*

It is always said that "the horse is the friend of man". He proves this by the fact that, although he is so much stronger, he lets *you*, little you, control him. In return he wants you to look after him. He knows that if you are really going to get the best out of him, you must be firm as well as kind.

Now that we have such wonderful modern inventions, especially in transport, there is really no need for horses and ponies for utilitarian purposes. We only keep them because they give us pleasure and we can have fun with them. So remember, *riding must always be fun*. If it is not, if you are nervous, if you get angry when you fall off or are beaten in a gymkhana or a show, if you get impatient when your pony does not learn as quickly as you would like—then give it up. Buy a bicycle or an autoscooter: it won't mind when you get angry. A pony will: and he will remember. Then, instead of being the means of giving you a great deal of pleasure, he will just be an annoyance, and soon will become vicious and nasty.

Finally, remember that although you may only be interested in one kind of horsemanship—jumping, or gymkhanas, or hunting—it does not mean that you should ignore the other kinds of horsemanship — dressage, showing or racing. All of us who love horses and ponies are one big family, and just like members of a family we should all be interested in each other's activities. Then, and only then, will we be united, a great family of horse-lovers, who can ensure the survival of horses and ponies, all the sports in which they feature and all the fun they give us if properly looked after.

We hope that you have enjoyed this book and that you will enjoy your riding more because of what you have learnt.